SEXUALITY: A CHRISTIAN VIEW
Toward Formation of Mature Values

Foreword by Bernard Häring, C.Ss.R.

SEXUALITY
A Christian View

Toward Formation of Mature Values

Rev. Gennaro P. Avvento, S.T.D.

Twenty-Third Publications
P.O. Box 180, Mystic, CT. 06355

Edited by Carol Clark
Designed by John G. van Bemmel
Cover by William Baker

Library of Congress Catalog Card Number 82-82387
ISBN 0-89622-158-x

Foreword

In recent years both professionals and non-professionals have done studies in the area of human sexuality. Yet, no treatment of human sexuality can be considered credible from a Christian perspective if it is not seen in the full light of revelation and in terms of human development. A defensive posture, an attitude of prohibition, a fortress mentality are no longer acceptable. Nor do we find acceptable an approach that sees sexuality as a series of problems to be solved neatly and individually. The area of sexuality, rather, must be seen as a mystery of covenant between God and humankind.

For this reason I endorse this work by my former student and friend, Fr. Avvento. His presentation of sexuality speaks a language of credibility; it unmasks the falsities of rigorism and laxism. As a scholarly work, it represents the ability to draw from many sources and to personalize them in a comprehensive and cogent message. To the author's credit, this work remains readable for the student, the teacher, and the concerned Christian adult.

The author's perspective is deeply incarnational, that is, it is rooted in the fact of the bodily presence of Jesus Christ in the world today. The belief that the human body is charged with the grace of the risen Christ governs the topics treated in this book. While the topics covered here are controversial, they are handled with sober reflection, academic honesty, and pastoral sensitivity. In this respect, the work represents a fine synthesis of mind and heart.

It is my hope that this book will serve as a vehicle to communicate the truth which is the person of Jesus Christ. Only an enlightened person can be free and only a free person can be responsible. Only a reflective and open church can be a positive force in the world, transforming the darkness of ignorance into the light of knowledge.

—Bernard Haring C.Ss.R.

Acknowledgments

A book can scarcely be considered the work of one person, working alone and without support. This particular book originated as a series of adult education lectures offered in 1978 at the parish of St. Catherine of Siena in Riverside, Connecticut. So overwhelming was the response to the topic that the ideas were gathered and used for course material at Marymount Manhattan College in 1980-81. The author is indebted to all of his students for their critical appraisal of the material, for without their insight and support this work in its present form would not have become a reality.

Before and during the preparation of the final manuscript, a number of people emerged as instrumental in the transformation of possibility into reality: Rev. Vincent J. O'Connor, pastor of St. Catherine's, who gave the author the freedom and trust so necessary to pursue this topic; Rev. Joseph LoCigno, who encouraged the author to refine his thoughts; Carol Clark, John van Bemmel, and Cathy Clark, who believed in this work and spent many hours preparing the text; June LaPegna, who sifted through many pages, corrected mistakes, and offered invaluable reflections on the work, both general and particular; Carol Gianisello, Carol Santora, and Emma Doring, who collated the many pages of text and enabled the author to keep his sense of humor and perspective in the many days of re-writing and re-editing. To you, my friends, this book is dedicated.

Contents

8   Responsible Parenthood   84

9   The Issue of Sterilization   90

16   Recent Issues in Bio-Medicine   156

Introduction

Today's society raises many questions regarding human sexuality that call for a Christian response. No one of us can escape the urgency of these issues because human sexuality embraces the entire person in every phase of his or her existence. As concerned believers take stands, however, they seem to be forming themselves into two distinct lines of battle, each pitted against the other with equal vehemence.

One group bears the standard, "God save the tradition!" In the field of sexual ethics these persons represent the parent figure. They persistently call upon the "reliable" moral theology of so-called "authoritative handbooks" to denounce both bad situations and persons alike. This textbook or manual tradition ignores or rejects the insights of contemporary sexual anthropology.[1]

On the other side are those whose battle cry is "Watch us radicals!" They stand for the child figure responding emotionally to the parental admonitions of the traditions.[2]

This sexual-ethics battlefield, at its best, offers a specific example of what theologian Bernard Lonergan, S.J. described as the general crisis occurring in Christian philosophy and theology: As these disciplines move from a classical to a modern cultural context, they become more existential and historical.[3] On the one side, a solid right wing has formed that is stubbornly determined to live in a world that no longer exists. On the other side, a scattered left wing moves erratically, captivated by every latest development, following one possibility after another.[4]

The Catholic heritage has never suffered from a lack of interest in the area of sexual ethics. This interest has spawned various traditions—some rich, some poor. Enduring allegiance to the ancient tabu concerning sex has guaranteed the dominance of the poor traditions. I claim, however, that authentic orthodoxy consists in a real fidelity to the great, living tradition. This fidelity requires one courageously to read anew, in the light of both science and faith, the experience of Christians from generation to generation. This true fidelity implies vigorous opposition to both parent and child games. Such foolish pastimes delay, and sometimes prevent the emergence of the authentic Christian adult.

1

The intention of this author is to offer a panoramic view of sexuality in contemporary society. I will then delve into specific areas, areas that are not only topical but crucial to self-understanding.

The advances and insights of philosophy and the empirical sciences will be brought to bear upon the Christian vision of faith, because any presentation on sexuality that ignores statistical data would be both vague and abstract—it would not accurately serve as a reflection of human experience. I have been careful, however, not to rely totally on statistical data. As priest-sociologist Andrew Greeley points out, "Mere statistics on the sexual behavior of males and females cannot be the final word on the subject."[5] Our approach strives to be a "valued" one that is consciously and explicitly directed to the moral growth and formation of the individual.

What I hope to offer, therefore, is an integrated vision of sexuality, a vision that is cogent as well as liberating, a vision that probes and yet remains within the realm of the authentic living tradition of the church.

1

Sexuality in the Contemporary Vision

We live in a sex-saturated society which tends to ignore any approach to sexuality that is personal and value-oriented. Constant reminders of this mindless, heartless brand of sex pollute the atmosphere in which we try to survive as sexual beings.

I. The Sex Saturation Package

The brand of sex "sold" in the marketplace has greatly affected our understanding of ourselves as sexual beings and our perception of the meaning of sexual relations.

A. Consumerism

Sex is, perhaps, the best-selling commodity on the open market.

The field of journalism boasts such publications as *Oui, Hustler, Club International, Penthouse, Forum, Playboy, Playgirl,* etc. Theater billboards in large cities and sedate suburbs capitalize on the public demand for the sexual product with such fetching titles as *Super Vixens, Peach Fuzz, Wild Country, Magnificent Sinner,* and *You Don't Have to Be Married.*

The media have capitalized on the use of sex not only for purposes of entertainment, but to sell products as well. One look at television commercials shows the viewer how far the selling of sex has come.

If one has a good product (sex *is* a good product), and you advertise it well, the product will sell. We have learned to package sex so pleasantly as to guarantee mass consumption of the product. The demand is great; the volume must adequately meet the demand: This is the simple economics of sex.

3

B. The Performance Mentality

Many today equate the term "sexuality" with sexual performance. The ability to perform well has become the measure of success and fulfillment within our society. Sex, seen as functional expertise, has become disassociated from the human dimensions of intimacy and relationship that are so vital to personal living. Viewed as an end-in-itself, sex is no longer valued as the supreme manner of interbodily and interpersonal communication. Men and women "rate" each other's ability to perform, and the craze is to base looks and performance on a numerical system in which *10* is the optimum. Many look hopefully to the day when we may perfect a sexual *Six Million Dollar Man* and *Bionic Woman.* With technological know-how pushed to the limit, why should a "love-machine" seem absurd?

While advertising has helped to sell sex as a product, the various and sundry sex-therapy clinics promise to enhance performance. In the 1960s a variety of learned and less-learned books and reports capitalized on the widespread interest in various aspects of sex and sexuality. Characterized by significant changes in customs, the decade ushered in a revolution in which sex was seen as both personal and social salvation.

In 1966 Masters and Johnson's carefully documented and purposely impersonal scientific research report, *Human Sexual Response,* exploded upon this charged societal atmosphere. While Kinsey opened the doors of contemporary culture to the study of human sexual response from the sociological point of view, this work moved the science of sexology forward by measuring in a laboratory setting the physiological and psychological sexual responses of men and women. This book was followed by the equally striking volume *Human Sexual Inadequacy.* This work used the clinical findings as the basis for treating sexual disfunctions. The approach marked a breakthrough for professional therapists.[1]

C. Refinement of the Pleasure Principle

The efficiency of the technological society in which we live has even transformed the world's oldest profession, prostitution. Prostitution in the form of "street-walking" is now looked upon as primitive. Today, massage parlors and pleasure palaces have added a touch of class to the selling of sex.

A very good commentary upon this transition can be found in Peter Whittaker's *The American Way of Sex.*[2] This book ex-

4

plores the confines of the massage parlors by presenting interviews with people who are employed in the business. The persons involved are highly educated, extremely articulate men and women who have succeeded in sophisticating the pleasure principle in our society. The client comes in, pays his fee, listens to soft music, picks his program, and then enters a world where he can engage in anything from conversation to intercourse. This is all "off the record," of course, since technically the customer is interested only in a massage. Parlor employees do very well: The working conditions are pleasant, the protection is good, and the money is excellent.

The entire philosophy of sex for pleasure is highlighted in these lines from a popular book of ten years ago:

> Sex is an evil when it is utilized for a purpose and not for pleasure. It is an evil when its single intent is to conceive children. This is delimiting to man. It thwarts, twists, stunts, and destroys him. It is the act of enchaining his strongest instinct and making it a slave to all manners of external demands, while all the while repressing that which must be given release and relief if man is to know himself and maintain his health.[3]

The pleasure principle as an end-in-itself has perhaps reached its apex in the philosophy of Hugh Hefner and *Playboy*. The philosophy of "playthingism" is one of expendable sex. Women and men have only a transient and functional value for each other. Everyone is capable of replacement. One can always "put on" another person, as one puts on clothing. And when the season is over, one either stores away these playthings for future use or throws them away like swim trunks in autumn or skis in the spring.

Such seasonal sex serves only a recreational need. With a playmate one may borrow the language of love, but any real affective commitment is to be avoided: Sex is only for fun, not for intimacy. The playmate is a packageable item on the consumer market, something to be bought, used, then thrown away. By way of critique, Theodore Roszak writes, "At a stroke, half the population is reduced to being the inconsequential entertainment of the technocracy's pampered elite."[4]

The final result of treating sex in this fashion is standardization. Erotic feelings become cliches and are sold like merchandise. The sexuality of men and women is limited and prefabricated. This exaltation of the stereotype is profoundly antisexual, depersonalizing and dehumanizing. Eugene Kennedy states in his book, *The New Sexuality: Myths, Fables, and Hangups:*

> Man likes to be reassured; that is the business of magazines like *Playboy* which is marvelously orchestrated to build a smooth but superficial shield of self-confidence around its readers. The true genius of *Playboy* rests on its capitalization of human uncertainty rather than on sexuality itself. It makes a man feel sophisticated.[5]

II. ANONYMOUS SEX

The secular vision of sexuality is based on a theme of anonymity. It results from a rift in the psychosexual identity of the person—in a disparity between his or her identity (*who* I am) and activity (*what* I do). This attitude prevents any intimacy or true interpersonal communication. Sexuality is reduced to sexual functioning and gratification of the sensual appetite.

This sense of anonymity is reflected in two general areas: pornography and sexual variation.

A. Pornography

It is generally agreed that the word pornography applies to certain pictures, publications, or films that show nudity or sexual activity in a way that violates contemporary standards of propriety.[6] The purpose of pornography is to excite people in some way, but experts disagree as to the long-range effects of this stimulation upon the individual and society.[7]

The actual word comes from the Greek *porne* meaning "whore" and *graphein* meaning "to write." The term literally means "to write to a whore." The analogy goes something like this: In prostitution one human uses another human as a sexual object. The person so used is presumably debased, and the user is humiliated by paying for something that one ought to be able to get for free. In pornography a human being uses an object as an object, but, as in prostitution, strictly for impersonal, nonthreatening sexual stimulation.[8]

Basically *hard-core* pornography offers visual satisfaction. The personality types who involve themselves in this milieu often are the victims of sexual inadequacy.[9] They flock to movies, peepshows, and magazine racks in the hope of satisfying a hunger that they cannot ordinarily satisfy within the framework of a dynamic interpersonal relationship.

The loners and low-lives who have never achieved sexual fulfillment in a love relationship roam the streets of our society with the burning desire to fill the void that tortures their souls. Pornography fills the emptiness, the loneliness. It provides the necessary stimulus and satisfaction to carry them through another day. This is both a sad and tragic commentary upon our contemporary society. The comical image of the dirty old man in the long raincoat who seeks his kicks in rundown theaters is all too true, but the protagonist in the contemporary scenario is often young, clean-cut, and rich.

B. SEXUAL VARIATIONS

Sex games have replaced charades as the modern form of adult entertainment. Ironically, these games in themselves are charades. We focus our attention here on three examples: sado-masochism, group sex, and mate-swapping.

1. Sado-Masochism The intriguing fantasy world of sado-masochism is gaining in popularity. Sundry sexual activities, divorced from person and from love, camouflage a tragic poverty of spirit, a lack of perception concerning sexual identity. The personality types who engage in this world are lonely or bored people who cannot communicate sexually and, therefore, are imprisoned by sex.

I recall one story that typifies the imprisonment that is experienced in the world of the sado-masochist. A boy was involved from an early age in a master-slave relationship with his mother. He was prodded, poked, pulled, chained, and tormented sexually until he grew to enjoy it. As an adult he now claims to have a good sexual relationship with his wife, but once a month he returns home to mother!

This story is not extraordinary; the behavior described has become rather common. While few may suspect the true extent of sado-masochistic activities and participants, this strange world is no longer hidden in the closet. The new pleasure palaces have sophisticated the performance of the "unreal" as a form of entertainment in their business establishments. Scenes reminiscent of Jean Genet's *The Balcony* occur over and over again in our major cities. The types who are involved in this world rarely have intercourse. Rather, they seek to be abused to the point of orgasm—and they pay very well for the service.

One also finds such practices as fetishism, transvestitism, voyeurism, exhibitionism. While some apologists term many of

7

these actions or states "variations," it seems incredible that they should be so viewed.[10] Most regard them as deviations, abnormalities.

Everytime one reads or hears of adventures that pertain to this deviant world, sex is never discussed in a human context. It is rather regarded as a phenomenon, an element that must be used so that the tensions of life can be endured. Often people with personality disorders reveal these difficulties most graphically on the level of sexual expression.[11]

2. Group Sex   The famous Roman orgies of the past have been sophisticated, but the basic qualities remain the same—anonymity and transiency. For a rather provocative look at the sexual mores of America in general and the group-sex scene in particular, one need only read the recent best-seller *Thy Neighbor's Wife* by Gay Talese. At the very heart of this world of play lies a hidden fear of communication, commitment, responsibility, creativity, attachment. Group orgies satisfy a recreational need, yet all the participants share a general fear of being discovered: To preserve anonymity, they do not look each other in the eye.

3. Mate-Swapping   This is suburbia's answer to boredom and routine. In this pastime, all too often, one's partner becomes a means of exchange or barter. A person borrows his friend's wife, for example, in the same way in which he would borrow a tool from the garage. The favor is then returned. Variety and diversity are achieved through manipulation.

III. THE LOSS OF INTIMACY

Those who sell sex must appeal to all customers, normal and abnormal alike. Their product, offered openly for public consumption, must satisfy the wants and whims of every customer as fully as possible. When sex becomes a commodity it loses the dimensions of intimacy and symbolism. Removed from the context of love, sex is a mystery vandalized. The loss of intimacy is the greatest danger that faces our society today.

A. Loss of Personal Meaning

The secular viewpoint that we have illustrated holds in little esteem the integral values of love, trust, fidelity, sensitivity, warmth, and truth. Sex as partnership, as sharing that goes beyond the genital level, means very little if anything at all. Diversity and variety are the keys to pleasure. And the appetite that must be satisfied has grown so voracious it seeks to fill itself at every turn. It does not matter when, where, or how, if a person wants to be pleased, he or she does whatever is necessary to achieve that goal.

Fragile interpersonal relationships are easily ruptured. The covenant or bond needed to unite two people in truth is rarely entered into today, even by those who pronounce wedding vows.

In summary, the secular view of sex and sexuality rests on a poor image of the human person. Rather than recognize sexuality as an integral element of human personality, the total worth of the person is reduced to his or her genital functioning.

Such a viewpoint negates the interpersonal dimension of sex that is the cornerstone of the Judaeo-Christian tradition. As Christians we believe that as human persons we have been created in our totality as images of God. We are called to make a free personal response to the self-communication of God in Jesus Christ.

If we deny the personal nature and ultimate call of man and woman then we reduce ourselves to brute nature. Sex is dehumanized. In the secular world sexuality has been replaced by the search for the greatest orgasm. The context for the sexual act has been bypassed as an unnecessary preliminary. This approach to sex is like reading the ending of a mystery story without having read the book itself. The story ceases to be a mystery.

B. Disregard of Sexual Norms

If there is no meaning to sex, there is no rational way of determining what is right and what is wrong. People who have enough intellectual honesty to reflect on their own diffused, and perhaps confused, ideas on human sexuality will realize that they more or less consciously draw a line somewhere. In so doing, even though the line be far off, they are postulating some sort of sexual meaning.

If one refuses to admit the notion of sexual meaning, then one must be ready for the practical consequences that follow. A sexual life that fosters hatred, despair, violence, isolation, manipulation, injustice, sadness, coldness, chauvinism, rejection, constraint, and deceit is certainly unchristian because it is anti-human and destructive. Sexuality must be rational and loving. It must unify the individual (body-spirit) and the human race (man-woman). What this means concretely for us today is something to be discovered, realized anew, re-invented as it were.

The quest continues. For each one of us in every generation, the integrated development of our sexuality is a lifetime project, the exact blueprint for which is nowhere to be found. Success can be measured by the genuinely human quality of our rational existence: Through our sexed being, do we really reach those whom we love in a caring, human way?

The inability of secular society to answer yes to this question indicates the failure to reach sexual meaning. We all have the task, therefore, as human beings and as Christians, to develop an ethic that will enhance the search, a framework that will allow us to find sexual meaning. It is to that task that we now turn our attention.

QUESTIONS FOR DISCUSSION

1. Do you think that the contemporary vision of sexuality is a reaction to a prior, repressive outlook? Discuss.

2. Recently many schools have included sex education among their courses. Beyond the communication of biological facts do you think that such a program should emphasize education in sexuality and values?

3. If sex is a form of communication, it can be called language. As such it must have a structure. In this respect, how do you see the role of rules of conduct?

2

Toward a Contemporary Christian Vision of Sexuality

It is almost impossible to define human sexuality with precision. The diversity of cultures and the conditions of history make it extremely difficult to announce any one ideal of sexual, conjugal, or familial relationship to which all must conform. Nevertheless, we must at least attempt to examine the foundations of human sexuality and its dynamics in personal relationships.

To root our vision of sexuality in an adequate theological framework we will explore the psychological, scriptural, philosophical, and moral themes that will yield the most fruitful results. We then will offer a symbolic vision of sexuality that will serve as the leitmotif for our study.

I. Toward a Psychological Ground of Sexuality

Much has been written about the relationship between psychology and sexuality. Just as there is a pluralism in theology and philosophy, so too there is a pluralism in psychology. Among psychological theories there is as yet no single, comprehensive approach to sexuality and development that is acceptable. What is more, since the human person is a polymorphic structure, there never will be a single concept, model, or method that exhausts our understanding of human nature. Nevertheless, the behavioral sciences can teach us much, especially in this area of sexuality.

As we examine psychological insights, we must remember, above all, that sexuality can be correctly understood only as a

11

dimension of the total personality; personality is the more basic concept. A sexual person is primarily a sexual *person*.[1]

To say a person is sexual means many things. It means being sexually differentiated (male or female). It also means being relational (other-oriented, incomplete in oneself, socially directed). Sexual existence is both corporeal and social.

Human sexuality, while similar to animal sexuality in terms of biological functioning, is not merely the expression of a lower nature, it is filled with possibilities beyond the simple potential for generation.[2]

A. Affective and Genital Sexuality

Sexuality, therefore, has two dimensions, the affective and the genital. Our own culture has reduced sexuality to the genital dimension which is primarily biological.

Sexuality, however, has a social, as well as a biological, aim. Many psychologists such as Jung, Adler, Maslow, Frankl, and Erikson, see socialization as the primary goal of one's sexual life.[3] This is a far cry from the secular goal of recreation or tension reduction.

The way we view the relative importance of the biological and the social aims of sexuality depends upon our basic understanding of the human person. Do we understand person only as a biological creature or also as a social creature? Do we recognize a goal for sexuality that transcends the biological functions?

If we are better to understand our sexuality we must look more closely at the affective dimension of our sexual lives, i.e. the totality of affection, friendship, and tenderness in our relationships. As Erik Erikson points out, this is the dimension exhibited in compassionate people who are not only able to socialize their sexuality but, in rare cases, universalize it.[4]

In order to develop this affective dimension of sexuality, to achieve socialization, a person must first confront biological and physiological drives in such a way that he or she can feel comfortable with genitality. Placing an emphasis on the affective current of our sexual lives in no way makes the genital side of sexuality insignificant. If the genital side of personality is repressed, it leads to an affectively inhibited person. We must strive for affective integration, not inhibition.[5] The affective-social current and the genital-psychological currents of our sexuality are distinct but not separate, different and yet related.

12

B. Sexuality and Self-Actualization

To clarify this relationship between the affective and genital dimensions of sexuality we introduce the concept of multiple motivation developed by Abraham Maslow.[6] The term refers to the fact that a conscious desire on our part is not necessarily one desire but may contain a multiplicity of elements or motivations. This conscious desire may be a channel through which other goals are being sought.[7] For example, while sexual desire may seem to be a need for genital relations, it may represent affective needs as well.

The concern among teen-age boys over penis size reveals a need to impress. Their boasting over how far they can go with girls shows a deep-seated need for acceptance. Among teen-age girls the concern over breast size is rooted in a deep-seated need for security and self-esteem. The sexual desire may, in fact, express a need to have one's masculinity or femininity affirmed, a need that is a real burden in our society.

People also tend to confuse the physical desire for sex with the affective desire for intimacy. We experience sexual desire and think that what we need is genital satisfaction when actually we are longing for closeness. According to both Maslow and Rollo May, the higher need in a person is the need for intimacy.[8] Genital intercourse is not the initial step in forming a relationship. Rather, it should serve as the deepening of intimacy and the culmination of one's striving for it. Genital intercourse is a paradox, not needed but intensely enjoyed, frequently enjoyed as a peak experience.

In light of the multiple levels of sexual desire it can be affirmed that genital abstinence is not harmful for self-actualizing people, i.e. those who are actively seeking the development of their total personalities.[9] Such persons are able to accept genital deprivation and still be at ease with themselves and their sexual lives. Deprivation becomes pathogenic only when a pathogenic undercurrent surfaces, for example, when deprivation is experienced as rejection by the opposite sex, as inferiority, as isolation. In such cases the desire for biological sex is masking deeper affective needs. The significant element in personal development is not genital abstinence in itself, but one's attitude toward it.

C. Femininity and Masculinity

Beyond the distinction between affective and genital sexuality lie questions pertaining to gender. We affirm that the human person exists as male or female. What does this mean?

13

To answer this question we must make an important distinction between maleness and masculinity, femaleness and femininity. We must also understand our psychological bisexuality, that is, the fact that none of us is purely male or female.[10]

Richard Stoller, basing his thought on data acquired at the Yale University Sex Therapy Clinic, distinguishes between "the sense of maleness/masculinity" and "the sense of femaleness/femininity."[11] The sense of maleness or femaleness is related to one's biology; it refers to a person's certainty that he or she belongs to one of the two sexes and is fixed easily in life by psychological as well as by biological determinants.

But the awareness "I am male" or "I am female" differs from the awareness "I am masculine" or "I am feminine." All things considered, masculinity and femininity are culturally established, not genetically determined.[12] Those qualities that a culture ascribes to a man or woman are not inherent in sexual differentiation itself. The so-called masculine qualities are not the exclusive prerogative of men nor are the positive qualities that a culture ascribes to a woman the exclusive property of women.

The famous psychologist Carl Jung alluded to this idea in his classical distinction between the *anima* and the *animus;* the *anima* is the femine dimension in man while the *animus* is the masculine dimension in woman.[13] Each person possesses both dimensions. Masculine and feminine sex roles, however, are influenced by child-rearing practices and the movement of socialization.[14]

When we talk about men and women we are talking about sexual differentiation; when we talk about femininity and masculinity we are talking about cultural stereotypes and socialized roles. The notion of psychological bi-sexuality does not affirm the validity of these roles and stereotypes but simply says that in the process of coming to sexual identity we have to deal with cultural stereotypes and social roles.

Our primary goal as human beings is to become persons, reflecting subjects.[15] We must learn to see sexuality, not in isolation, but in the context of this personalization process: The person each seeks to become is a male person or a female person. It is the nonpersonal approach that leads to sexism.[16]

Maleness or femaleness is not something we know *a priori.* What it means to be a man or woman is something we discover in relationships. And although we can discover many aspects of our sexuality in relationships with members of our own sex, we can fully understand what it means to be a man or woman only vis-a-vis

14

the other sex.[17] There is no male or female essence that we can pin down. We need others to help us find out who we are and we especially need the other sex in this task of self-discovery.

Being a man means experiencing something that a woman will never experience. A woman, for example, will never experience the anxiety that accompanies a boy's first physical arousal or his embarrassment in walking down a public street with a noticeable erection. And a man will never experience the monthly period, child-bearing, breast-feeding, and motherhood.

Each of us has to learn to be comfortable with who he or she is and to separate self-worth from cultural definitions. We must differentiate our personal growth from cultural expectations if we are to become the persons we freely choose to be.

Sexual differentiation involves the concepts of manhood and womanhood as well as those of masculinity and femininity. Both of these are distinct but interrelated tasks of sexual identity.[18] It is important for sexual identity that the woman has a sense of femaleness and the man has a sense of maleness.

D. Sexual Attraction

The principal difference between human persons and the lower animals is the extent to which sexual arousal is affected by symbolic factors. Sexual attraction is not so much a question of drives and instincts. Rather sexual arousal in a man or woman results from a combination of hormonal readiness and external symbolic stimuli—neither is sufficient without the other.[19]

Sexual arousal needs to be clearly distinguished from love. Sexual attractions and desires, on the one hand, do not necessarily imply love for another person by whom we are aroused: Sexual attraction can be experienced apart from love and affection. Love, on the other hand, may remain when sexual attraction diminishes or it may exist without the presence of felt sexual forces. The true adult can differentiate between sexual desire and genuine love. This is not to say that genuine love is not sexual; it simply means that not all that is sexual is love.[20]

Sex is not a panacea for human problems, although people do look to the sexual world for salvation. Many of the problems that confront us are not due to the fact that we are celibate or single or married but to the fact that we are living human beings. While part of us wants to cling to the fairy tale of eternal bliss, the adult portion of our personalities knows the world as it is.

The realization of our sexual identity is a lifelong process of personal growth and integration. This 'process is not simply biological; it is also religious and moral. Only against a spiritual backdrop can we properly see the goal toward which we strive. It is to this backdrop we now turn.

II. SACRED SCRIPTURE AND HUMAN SEXUALITY

Do the scriptures have anything to offer regarding the mystery of sexuality in general and sexual behavior in particular? Although there are many allusions to sexuality in sacred scripture, the bible is not concerned with sexuality as such. This general statement requires clarification.

According to *Human Sexuality,* the much debated report from the Catholic Theological Society of America (CTSA), the bible should not be seen as giving absolute and universal prescriptions with regard to sex.[21] Obviously, specific, culturally conditioned statements cannot claim validity for all time. Yet I would maintain, contrary to the authors, that although all human discourse is limited by time and context, this does not mean we should dismiss the wisdom of other times and places out of hand. While it is true that limitations are imposed by the historical and cultural context in which statements are originally made, not all biblical instructions fall in the same category.[22] We have to employ a sound mode of interpretation to avoid denying the possibility of lasting validity for any revealed statement. The CTSA report tends to be simplistic and overly general in this regard.

The scriptures are not intended to give a systematic presentation on sex; they are not a textbook on ethics.[23] One cannot find in the bible prefabricated ethical models for sexual behavior any more than one can find these ethical models for medicine, nuclear warfare, civil rights, etc. Yet, if we are attuned to the various social and cultural movements represented in scriptural statements, we may discover the foundation of an ethical tradition that will suggest certain models of behavior. Unfortunately, the CTSA report fails to be attentive to these traditions.[24]

While the bible does not provide us with a simple "yes" or "no" code of sexual ethics, most scholars would agree that sacred scripture in its totality regards sexuality as one aspect of life, properly viewed only within the context of the whole person and the whole of human life with all its relationships and responsibilities.

The Old Testament contains such a plurality of customs, laws, and insights related to sexuality that no single voice can be said to prevail. However, contrary to the CTSA report, both the patriarchal and prophetic traditions offer key insights into fundamental sexual themes and developments within the people of Israel.

As in the Old Testament, the New Testament also reflects certain historical conditioning. While it cannot be said that Jesus proposed a new and unified sexual ethic, nevertheless he did make a breakthrough in his essential teaching on the equality of man and woman, his prohibition of divorce, and his affirmation of the law of love.

Contemporary biblical scholarship makes it clear that we cannot validly abstract statements regarding sexuality from their biblical contexts and then use them as proof texts to validate any twentieth century theology of human sexuality. I would maintain that the CTSA report falls victim to this deductive approach and reflects the same mistake that plagued the manuals of moral theology of an earlier era.

Sacred scripture is not at fault if it fails to answer certain problems and questions regarding premarital intercourse, masturbation, birth regulation, etc. These questions just were not asked then to the extent that we ask them today. Yet, they were asked in a certain way, at times implicitly and at times explicitly. Biblical scholarship must be very careful to analyze this empirical data to discover whether or not certain sexual acts were indeed approved or rejected in an absolute way.

The bible provides us with certain fundamental themes, certain guidelines and prohibitions, that can serve as a basis for constructing a contemporary theology of human sexuality. These themes will emerge as part of our groundwork for the moral evaluation of sexual conduct.

III. A THEOLOGICAL APPROACH TO SEXUALITY

Among the plurality of theological expressions in the world today I have found the personalist approach yields the most accurate portrait of sexuality in conformity with the psychological, scriptural, and historical data.

A. Sexuality as Comprehensive Human Gift

Sexuality must be numbered among the essential determining factors in human nature. It characterizes the entire structure of a human being as man or woman and affects the behavior of the individual as regards mental attitudes and processes. According to the most recent statement of the Roman Catholic Sacred Congregation for the Faith:

> It is from sex that the human person receives the characteristics which, on the biological basis, the psychological and spiritual levels, make that person a man or woman and thereby largely condition his or her progress towards maturity and insertion into society.[25]

Sexuality is a force that permeates, influences, and affects every act of a person's being at every moment of existence. It is not just operative in one restricted area of life (e.g. genital functioning), but is rather at the core and center of our personal life-response. As I have already mentioned, sexuality is not just something added to human nature, it is that which determines a person as man or woman.

Human sexuality is a fundamental modality by which we relate to ourselves, to other people, and to God. We always exist and function as sexual persons; at no time is our sexuality not a part of us. The gift of sexuality is thus a wholistic or comprehensive gift.[26]

The scriptural vision of the book of Genesis serves as a starting point for this vision of sexuality as gift. The two different accounts of creation (Yahwist 950 B.C. and Priestly 550 B.C.) both take a unitary view of the human race. In this vision man is neither "he" nor "she." "Man" is male and female. It is by the loving dialogue between man and woman that the image of God is realized, that men and women become truly human.[27] The Old Testament makes no suggestion that maleness or femaleness is the result of some primeval fall from innocence as do the mythologies and cults of the ancient near-eastern world.[28] Sexuality can be described as something freely created by God, an aspect of our nature of which human beings need never be embarrassed or ashamed in any way.

In the bible, sex is never isolated, but always seen in the context of the whole person. The Yahwist tradition sets the sexual nature of men and women within the framework of our nature as social and relational beings (Genesis 2:18). Within this vision

18

mutuality is the primary purpose of sex, and the monogamous couple is presented as the ideal. Sex is seen as a gift from God moving people from loneliness to relationship (Genesis 2:24). On the other hand, the Priestly tradition reveals that sexuality is related to procreation, a sharing in God's activity and dominion over life.

Above all, the book of Genesis refuses to "divinize" sex, for Yahweh stands beyond the polarity of the sexes. Israel's fundamental creed, monotheism, was the most decisive element in the elaboration of a Jewish sexual ethic. No other god or goddess could be associated with Yahweh.[29] Sexuality was thus desacralized and assumed its properly secular reference. The role of archetype was no longer exercised by the sexuality of the gods. Rather, human beings such as Adam and Eve served as prototypes. This is well expressed by the famous Old Testament theologian, Gerhard von Rad:

> But, for the historian of religion what is most astonishing is Yahwism's self-preservation vis-a-vis the mythicizing of sex. In the Canaanite cult, copulation and procreation were mythically regarded as a divine element; consequently the religious atmosphere was as good as saturated with mythical sexual conceptions. But Israel did not share in the "divinization" of sex. Yahweh stood absolutely beyond the polarity of sex, and this meant that Israel also could not regard sex as a sacral mystery. It was excluded from the cult because it was a phenomenon of the creature.[30]

From the experience of Genesis we see how sexuality is truly a human mystery, that is, it is part of the God-given nature of man and woman. The uniqueness of Israel remained in the fact that these people did not involve God in the mythology of carnal commerce.

B. Sexuality as Relational

By way of broad definition, human sexuality is that way of being in and relating to the world as a male or female person. Sexuality is the mode or manner by which human beings experience and express both the incompleteness of their individualities as well as their relatedness to each other as male and female.[31] This definition goes beyond a limited understanding of sexuality as genital and generative functioning.

From a theological point of view, human sexuality is the concrete manifestation of the divine call to completion, a call extended to every person in the very act of creation and rooted in the very call of his or her being. From the first moment of existence our

19

sexuality summons us to intrapersonal and interpersonal growth.[32] On the intrapersonal level we are called to be that man or woman that each can become while on the interpersonal level we are called to reach out to others.

Sexuality is not just an isolated biological or physical phenomenon accidental to human beings, but rather an integral part of personal self-expression and self-commitment to others.

Sexuality is a profound good given to us by God. It should be accepted as a characteristic of our very humanity and used to facilitate human growth toward identity and maturity. As a Christian, I envision this call to maturity as a call to personal growth in Christ.

As I have already mentioned, by means of a person's sexual identity he or she experiences incompleteness and dependence upon another person. The completion we seek will be fully realized on the eschatological level when we become one in the "Other" who is God.[33]

Since sexuality is grounded in the center of human personality, its actuation affects the entire person. The framework of the primary sexual relationships is that of a triad. It originates with *eros,* a desire for another based on personal need. Gradually an affection and love may develop that is directed to the entire person of the other and accepts the other not merely for the sake of one's own need but also because one loves the other person in himself or herself (*philia*). This acceptance will correspond freely and fully to the dignity of the other person, however, only if it surpasses narcissistic self-love, and is joined to a love that gives itself (*agape*), a love that is prepared to make sacrifices and is directed to the "you" of the other, a love that is a reflection of that love which God has for each of us.[34]

C. Sexuality as Embodiment

From the perspective of existential phenomenology I make the following distinction: "I am my body" and not "I have a body." This is one way of saying that all levels of consciousness are touched by our embodied presence in the world.[35]

Sexuality in this view is that aspect of our bodily "being-in-the-world" whereby we are present and open to that which is not ourselves, to that which is "other" than ourselves. Embodied subjectivity reaches out to another body-subject in order to banish loneliness and to experience the fullness of "being-with-another" in the human project.

As a result, for human beings any teleology of the pleasure bond should be seen as an intercourse of subjectivities and not just as a tension-reducing experience. It is more than copulation and orgasm; it is not just the striving for biochemical equilibrium. In the genital union, in the intertwining of subjectivities, the fullest potential of human realization can be reached. And yet, despite the unity and ecstasy of the moment, the partners remain distinct.

On this point we offer some clarification in terms of the thought of Saint Paul. It seems that he had been unjustly accused of an antipathy toward the sexual impulse and toward the body in general. More accurately, Saint Paul was a realist who had no illustions about the actual condition of men and women. Regarding sex he was very much a Jew of his day, namely, he saw sex as a fact of creation which, therefore, is good (I Corinthians 7:5). But since he believed that this world was soon to pass away he felt it would be better to remain unmarried. (I Corinthians 7:26-27). Seen in the perspective of the kingdom, absolute continence is a good, a greater good even than the lawful use of marriage, for those who have the gift for such a vocation.[36]

Saint Paul's warnings against the inclinations of the flesh (Romans 8:6) and the works of the flesh (Galatians 5:19) are not to be understood as a condemnation of embodiment. The word "flesh" meant something quite different for Saint Paul than it does for us. The Old Testament used the term to designate all that is temporal, all that passes, all that is weak, corruptible, and, therefore, mortal. The biblical notion of flesh embraces the total human sphere, the total person with all his or her physical and mental corruptibility. Saint Paul's references to the flesh are by no means synonymous with the body understood as materiality.[37] He does not wish to contrast the material body of the human person with the spiritual component or soul. The reading of a platonic dualism into the biblical ideas of spirit and flesh has led, in the past, to a false ascetical ideal in which the body was despised and holiness was identified with the rejection of physical pleasure, including the pleasure of sex.[38]

In view of what we have said here, we can see that sexuality serves the development of human persons by calling them to constant creativity, to full openness to being, to the realization of every potential within the personality, to a continued discovery and expression of authentic selfhood. While procreation is one reason for sexual expression on the genital level, it is not the only one. Sexuality as it is lived in bodily existence is God's own way of calling people out of themselves and into relationships with others.

21

D. Sexuality as Personal Communication

It is imperative that, as human beings, we locate our sexuality within a human perspective. We cannot view sexuality outside of our personal identity. Our personalities are not merely a bare material that we mold. They are a gift given to us by God and as such must be cherished and allowed to grow.

The exercise of sexuality can take on many styles and show itself in many ways—a smile, a kiss, a hug, a handshake, the way one thinks, acts, and reacts, etc. Always involved is the desire to communicate with our bodies that we feel in our hearts and minds. We communicate by signs. Thus, sexual signs are both unitive and communicative. [39]

On the genital level, the deepest expression of love that can take place between two humans is the act of intercourse. The very biological structure of a human being points to the fact that the act is geared toward unity and communication. The male organ is designed for penetration, while the female is designed for active receptivity. The mystery of sex is such that body chemistry must be at work if the act is to be performed. Only when the partners are ready can intercourse take place. The very transformation that takes place (erection in the male and vaginal lubrication in the female) attests to this. When both partners are ready there is a certain harmony and rhythmic pattern as the two become one.

IV. The Growth of the Personalist Perspective

Within our particular century the general thrust of the official Christian viewpoint on sexuality and marriage has been contained (one might say enshrined) in these words taken from the Code of Canon Law: *The primary purpose of marriage is the procreation and education of children. The secondary purpose of marriage is the mutual support of the couple and a remedy for concupiscence.* [40]

The personalist perspective of sexuality did eventually emerge with clarity, but only after much struggle. Through the courageous writing of theologians such as Hubert Doms, Bernhardin Krempel, and Dietrich von Hildebrand this vision gradually gained support despite the fact that it was at times obscured by official statements of the church.

Vatican II took a step forward when it insisted on the inseparable connection between the two purposes of marriage and suggested the consideration of the human person as the source of integration. The *Pastoral Constitution on the Church (Gaudium et Spes)* describes conjugal love as the foundation of marriage, the bond between man and woman that serves as the basis for marriage as a sacrament:

> This love (conjugal) is eminently a human one since it is directed from one person to another through an affection of the will. It involves the good of the whole person. Therefore it can enrich the expressions of body and mind with a unique dignity.[41]

The decade of the 1960s marked the decisive turning point in the attitudes and practices of many Catholics regarding sexuality. Several factors precipitated this shift on both the theological and nontheological levels.

One such factor was the person-oriented approach to morality ushered in by developments in biblical, historical, and systematic theology. New insights into personal identity and sexuality resulting from advances in the behavioral and social sciences, also had considerable effect. These gains touched the general population leading to a growing appreciation of the dignity of the individual and the value of personal freedom, individual conscience, and responsibility.

Some of these factors influenced one of the most recent statements on sexuality, *Persona Humana,* issued in 1975. This declaration, while still a product of a classical world view, shows an advance in the personalist orientation. It contains some keen insights that provide solid ground for a personalist vision of sexuality. On the practical level this statement follows the tradition closely by treating specific sexual questions in terms of a simple objective-subjective framework. On the theoretical level, however, it develops the past tradition substantially. Instead of presenting human sexuality merely in the context of marriage, it recognizes it to be radically rooted in the very nature of the human person and important to growth at every stage of being.

This view has been most recently stressed and developed by the National Committee for Human Sexuality Education in their publication, *Education in Human Sexuality for Christians.*[42]

Key points highlighted in this document, are basic to the vision that has shaped this book. The reader can relate all that follows to these convictions of the author:

1. Genuine moral behavior comes from internal conviction rather than external coercion.

2. Jesus Christ is the ultimate norm of all morality.

3. The nature of the human person provides the proximate norm for determining appropriate moral behavior.

We next turn to a deeper look at the human person in responsible relation to the community.

4. The role of personal conscience is critical in the determination of particular moral behavior.

5. There is no single universal code of human behavior that is applicable to all circumstances and peoples.

6. The church, as an institution, must be attentive to the psycho-social currents in society and not seek to regulate behavior in a cultural vacuum.

QUESTIONS FOR DISCUSSION

1. Jot down characteristics you associate with masculinity. Make a similar list of feminine characteristics. Where did your ideas concerning masculinity and femininity originate?

   Place a check mark next to qualities in each list that you believe you possess. Reflect on the results or discuss them with others. Can you relate your self-portrait to anything you have read in this chapter?

2. This chapter indicates that sacred scripture is not an ethical codebook containing specific "dos" and "don'ts" regarding sexual and other behavior. Instead the bible offers insights into fundamental sexual themes. Recall some of these themes discussed in this chapter. How can these insights guide us in making particular decisions? Give an example.

3. Look over the official church statements included in this chapter. Do you see these statements reflected in church teaching and practice at the parish level? Discuss. Give examples.

3

Conscience, Values, and Sexual Behavior

I. Conscience and Personal Identity

Many small children are familiar with the story of Jiminy Cricket who always tells Pinocchio to let his conscience be his guide. As children grow toward adulthood they often continue to think of conscience as a "little voice" whispering in the ear. The church, sensitive to the experience that prompts this simplistic view, describes the ultimate moment of decision-making as "being alone with God whose voice echoes in our depths."[1]

A. Fundamental Conscience

Conscience, however, is much more than a guide in decision-making. On a more fundamental level this power can be understood as self-consciousness in the fullest sense of that term. As we have already shown, we become conscious of our "selves" as persons by relating to others. As we grow in this awareness of self as involved in personal relationships with God and others, it becomes clearer to us what we are invited and obliged to do.

We are persons who have been given life by God as a gift or talent to be developed. We are called into dialogue with this personal God who is Father/Mother. Through faith we know Jesus Christ who invites us to become truly human. Gospel values guide us as we move toward this goal in union with others.

Conscience in the fuller sense has a broader role which we might term "intuitive." This term refers to the fact that, in a new moral situation, a sensitive person is receptive and open to the good even before he or she knows the rules concerning what ought to be done. This sense of "rightness" may come upon a person all at once, but usually it is the kind of knowledge that one receives gradually, and, perhaps, never very clearly. One may "see" value without ever being able to define precisely what is "seen." This ability often develops through experiences of contrast: We contrast a lived experience with Gospel values and this reflection reveals to us what is to be done in a given situation.

Conscience is more than intuitive, however; it is also functionally specific. That is, it operates in every concrete situation when we say to ourselves "I ought" or "I ought not." The sense of obligation is focused on a more personal level: It is *I* who "ought" or "ought not." We make a practical judgment regarding what has to be done.

When we move beyond this level and consider the role of the Holy Spirit in conscience we must be especially careful not to postulate the "little voice" theory. We have been given by God the ability to become informed, to reason, to love, to decide, to commit ourselves. The Spirit respects these gifts too much to render their exercise unnecessary. He does not plant commands in our minds as though we were robots. Conscience itself is not a means by which God "forces" human beings to obey laws or apply them. Rather, the Spirit frees us so that we can be interiorly present to ourselves. The Spirit works to release our persons from bondage into freedom. The Spirit helps us to know what to do here and now by making us aware of who we really are and who we want to become. Once we are in touch with our true selves, we encounter the indwelling presence of God at that inner center of our persons. The insight into who we are and what we must become inevitably leads us to what we are to do.

The Christian recognizes that the inner call to grow to maturity is a call from God, a call from Christ. Through the intuitive insight that reflection on the Gospel and life provide, the believer can discover what this call entails in the most concrete situations. The person can come to know that he or she is being called to follow a certain path in order to enflesh faith, hope, and love. The ultimate moment of realization is what we call conscience. Every human person forms and follows conscience in an autonomous manner, but always with the help of grace and under the light of the Gospel.[2] Conscience is formed by us; it does not fall from the heavens like manna.

B. The Right to Follow Personal Conscience

We affirm that a human being finds fulfillment by following his or her personal conscience. Without a doubt, the freedom to form and follow one's conscience constitutes a fundamental human right. If these rights are harmed, then the person is gravely injured because this is an attack on the deepest level of the self.

This truth was affirmed in no uncertain terms at Vatican II in the *Declaration on Religious Freedom*.[3] This document states that a person has the right to act according to his or her conscience and cannot be forced to act otherwise, even if that conscience is invincibly erroneous. The basis for these rights is, ultimately, the dignity of the human person.[4]

The Christian person who, in his or her "heart of hearts" stands directly before God in Christ, is accepted and responsible. But does a person have an unlimited right to follow personal conscience in the performance of external acts? For example, can a person who professes to act in good faith or from religious motives murder, steal, take his own life, or commit bodily harm to someone else?

To answer this question we must first note that the rights of human persons are, generally speaking, not absolute. They make up part of the whole spectrum of rights in society.[5] We cite the classical example: Can parents who are Jehovah's Witnesses be obliged to allow a blood transfusion for their children even though they view this as contrary to their religious beliefs? American legal codes do not permit the following of personal conscience in such situations. To allow this freedom would violate the established rights of other people, or cause grave social harm. Christian moral principles recognize similar limitations on personal rights. What are some of these principles?

First, a person who follows his or her erroneous conscience without injuring others should not be prevented from acting, unless the decision seriously compromises his or her welfare. For example, should not parents and society prevent children and adolescents from taking heroin or LSD? Based upon Christian standards, genuine human self-fulfillment will never involve mutilation or suicide. Prevention of these may provide the person with an opportunity to grasp more accurately the true direction of this personal fulfillment.

Second, if a person's erroneous conscience would lead him or her to injure others, he or she should be prevented from performing the external deed. The person in error has no right to injure other people. It is not a question of one right giving way to a stronger right; rather only one right is involved, the right of other persons to their own welfare, founded on the virtue of justice. A person in erroneous conscience has no unlimited right to sell pornographic material, to steal for a supposedly worthy cause, to commit perjury. Those actions have social ramifications that civil authorities may lawfully impede: The common welfare of the citizenry must be defended.

Third, one may not morally coerce or persuade another to act contrary to his or her own conscience. If a person remains convinced of a certain course of action despite all arguments to the contrary, he or she should follow this conviction and not be impeded.

II. MORAL NORMS

Moral theology asserts that the human person is responsible to exercise right human reason in concrete situations. Reason is the key that enables each of us to determine what is good and to act upon it. But, while this moral task of the individual is to be recognized and respected, human society still requires and, therefore, creates, norms stated as universals. The "universality" of such norms is, however, restricted in scope.

A. The Role of Universal Norms

While I strongly maintain the validity of such universal ethical statements, these statements always remain formal in the sense that they do not indicate the permissability of specific actions.[6] For example, to say that we are to do the good and to avoid the evil is a formal and universal statement of our ethical self-understanding that can be applied to every sphere of life, but the statement in itself does not tell us what is "good" and what is "evil" in a particular situation.

Our basic ethical self-understanding can be further specified in the form of transcendental norms that state ideals without describing the particular actions that lead to the realization of those ideals. For example Christians are directed to base their lives on faith, hope, love, and discipleship, but these universal imperatives say nothing about the concrete actions that express these virtues.[7]

When making a decision in a concrete situation we are called upon to choose from among several values or ideals the one that seems to us to take priority at the given time. Sometimes it is not merely a matter of choosing the greatest good from among many. Instead the values among which we must choose may be in conflict with one another.

As a result specific moral norms can never be so precise as to accommodate every possibility. When applying such norms our decisions will necessarily be influenced by the actual experience involved, the factual options recognized in a given society, and our specific self-understanding.[8]

B. Re-evaluation of Norms

We must finally realize that moral consciousness is never a solely individual experience but, rather, draws its substance from the community. This community has the task of discernment. Since the process of discernment can both uncover new insights and lead to error, continuing re-evaluation of existing norms is always necessary.

It can be shown, especially in the area of sexuality, that in the past faulty evaluations were made and false norms were established. If such was the case in the past, the same can be true in the present. And, since it is we ourselves, limited human persons, who formulate moral norms, we must avoid stating them as general or universal principles.

Finally, it must be remembered that the moral task proper to human persons is not to fulfill norms. If that were the case, our real life experiences would be a mere acting out of previously established moral values. Our task as Christian persons, however, is rather to discover moral values by seeking to christianize each life situation in which we are involved. This is a creative and redemptive work, a participation in the work of God who calls us to assist him.

C. Moral Norms as Pedagogical

As we have stressed, the moral task of the Christian is not to follow norms, but to christianize each life situation. Norms of behavior provide a pedagogical service; they guide us in fulfilling this responsibility.[9]

Since these norms are general in nature, they cannot give concrete direction to meet every situation. Nor do they tell us in precisely which situations they do apply. In a word, norms do not free us from the responsibility of making personal judgments. Yet, despite their limitations, norms are indispensable on the practical level—without them community living would be impossible.

Norms are especially helpful at times when an individual is not entirely capable of finding his or her own way. It is important to note, however, that it is precisely in such instances that norms are liable to be understood and lived as law or taboo with disregard for their proper limits.[10]

Our real task as Christians is to transform life itself. The moral mandate is to take each given situation and make of it something worthy of human persons. To do this requires more than rule-keeping, it is a work calling for creativity and commitment. Guided by this vision of the Christian vocation, we can learn to judge which of our shaping actions are truly human and, at least implicitly, begin to recognize which norms are involved in our decisions. By reflecting carefully on the experienced reality we can gradually come to appreciate the full meaning of the norms themselves.

We are moving toward a future when we will require fewer and less-detailed behavioral norms to guide us in performing the many specific tasks that contribute to the shaping of the world in accord with the Christian vision. We will be guided instead by fundamental principles which reflect a developed insight and heightened sense of responsibility in regard to the human and Christian task.[11]

III. CHRISTIAN MORAL MEANING AND VALUES

Behavioral norms can help us in the continuing search for moral meaning. We know, for example, that sexuality should be relational and loving, as well as integrative of the individual who is man-woman/body-spirit.[12] A sexual life that fosters hatred, despair, violence, isolation, manipulation, injustice, sadness, coldness, chauvinism, rejection, constraint, deceit, or any such nonvalues is certainly not Christian, because it is destructive of humanity.

But the correct application of these principles to real situations today is something that must be discovered, reinvented, indeed, realized anew. We must be able to distinguish the changeable from the unchangeable, the accidental from the essential, as the *Pastoral Constitution (Gaudium et Spes)* notes: *The church maintains that beneath all changes there are many realities which do not change and which have their ultimate foundation in Christ, who is the same yesterday and today, yes and forever.*[13]

That is the reason why the intervention of the magisterium of the Catholic Church in moral matters is not to be viewed as an intrusion or an attempt at domination. The tradition of the church, which is certainly expressed in the whole Christian life, is stated in a privileged and decisive way by the magisterium, This official teaching of the church is intended to help all people understand the divine message of revelation and its impact on life, to grasp what respect for human dignity requires at a given time, and, in short, help them discern the application of the natural law and the law of the Gospel.[14]

A. Moral Evil

How do we determine if an action is morally evil and, therefore, not to be done? Is every evil a moral evil?

Many actions in life, for one reason or another, significantly fail to reach the full potential of human goodness and possibility. Before judging these actions to be seriously evil, however, we must consider the context. Moral evil exists when there is not a proportionately good reason for permitting or even causing the actions to occur.

No single human act ever realizes the fullness of human possibility. All human acts contain within them elements of nongood. In most cases these minor imperfections are taken for granted. In other human actions, however, the lack of good is much more significant. The non-good or evil that attaches itself to all human acts has traditionally been termed physical evil.[15] This term, however, has led to confusion, especially when the non-good is not of a physical nature. The term ontic evil or premoral evil suggests more accurately that we are not referring to an evil about which a moral judgment is to be made.[16]

To determine whether an action contains a premoral evil or is a morally evil action, we must look not to the action alone, but to the action in its total context. The concepts of intrinsic moral evil and objectively grave moral evil are useful only when the action is considered in its total concrete reality. They cannot be used, as they were in the past, to judge an action apart from its context. Today we would say that the moral truth of an action stems only in part from its end and circumstances. The morality of an action is never determined from the object of the act alone.[17] Rather, the object, end, and circumstances of an action are part of a continuum. Moral evil is never determined by one of these factors apart from the other two.

B. Good and Bad Actions

How do we judge whether a particular action is morally good or evil? When the action is done to achieve a bad end, then the existence of moral evil is obvious. But suppose the person per-

31

forming the action has a good purpose. Due to some circumstances however, that purpose can be achieved only by performing an action that either contains significant degrees of premoral evil or leads to other results that contain significant degrees of premoral evil. In these cases the use of the category of proportionate reason is the best way to assess whether the premoral evil is actually a moral evil.[18] Proportionate reason asks: When one looks at the total action in context are there factors that make the level of premoral evil reasonably acceptable? If so, the act is not to be considered a moral evil. If such factors are not present, the act would be a moral evil.

In applying the category of proportionate reason, one cannot claim that an act is proportionate and free of moral evil simply because the individual doing the act thinks that he or she has a proportionate reason. Some individuals innocently fail to see the moral evil in their acts and are thus subjectively not responsible for the evil done. But the subjective judgment of these nonculpable persons does not change the objective immorality of the action.[19] Such persons should be challenged to recognize the flaw in their reasoning.

But what of absolute moral precepts? They can hardly be disregarded. In applying these precepts, however, the particular action must be considered in its totality. God does at times call a person absolutely to do this and not that in a specific situation. It does not follow, however, that the absolute moral obligation of this individual in this circumstance can be applied to all other cases involving the same act.[20]

The premoral evil so dominates some actions that it is virtually impossible to conceive of concrete cases where circumstances would morally justify them. Concerning such actions we can formulate virtually exceptionless or virtually absolute moral values that apply to all cases in which the acts occur.[21]

IV. Foundations of a Renewed Sexual Morality

The much debated CTSA report *Human Sexuality* offers a renewed approach to behavioral questions of human sexuality. According to the report, wholesome sexuality is that which fosters creative growth toward integration. Destructive sexuality results in personal frustration and alienation.[22]

A. Criteria for Sexual Behavior

According to the CTSA report, sexual integration includes values that are self-liberating, other-enriching, honest, faithful, socially responsible, joyous, and life-serving. The authors maintain that these values are essential to understanding and evaluating sexual behavior.

1. Self-liberating The sexual relationship cannot be spoken of exclusively as a totally altruistic giving of self to the other.[23] Wholesome self-interest is also involved. The proper exercise of human sexuality contributes to self-assurance, thereby enhancing a person's potential for growth and self-expression. But in affirming these values the authors of the CTSA report confuse the concepts of self-liberation and self-fulfillment. Self-liberation suggests the breaking of the bonds of false identity or negative self-image. Self-fulfillment, on the other hand, suggests arriving at a certain peace with the self, a certain identity, dynamic still, but rooted in confidence. The authors seem to forget that these global values can often be rationalized to soothe the conscience of the individual. They overlook the human potential for manipulation, egocentrism, and, above all, personal sin.

2. Other-enriching This quality calls for more than non-manipulation or non-exploitation of others against their wills. Wholesome sexuality must positively contribute to the growth process of the other.[24] It should be sensitive, considerate, thoughtful, compassionate, understanding, and supportive. It can be noted that the quality of enriching others should characterize not only our specifically sexual behavior, but all aspects of Christian living.

3. Honest Wholesome sexual expression implies mutual trust. Any pretense, evasion, or deception is a betrayal of that trust. To foster honesty in a relationship is difficult.[25] The whole issue of interpersonal communication is involved.

4. Faithful Fidelity facilitates the development of stable relationships. Yet, this emphasis on the uniqueness of the bond between two people, even in marriage, should not isolate the partners from all other relationships, thereby opening the way to jealousy.[26]

Fidelity, as the fulcrum for a plethora of moral values, is not adequately developed in the CTSA report. The covenant relationship between God and his people echoes in the covenant relationship between man and woman. Fidelity is the first fruit of life-commitment. The faithful person goes beyond loyalty or constancy and moves to the level of faith.[27] Fidelity is more than not committing adultery. It is an attitude, a moral leitmotif that serves as one's fundamental option in a life based on an ethic of responsibility.[28]

5. Socially responsible Since human beings are by nature social, it is only fitting that the creative and integrative forces of sexuality be exercised in the best interests of the larger community, i.e. family-nation-world.[29] We are called to exercise our sexuality in a way that reveals an awareness of the societal implications of our behavior. We are to act in a manner that is humbly and humanly constructive. Social responsibility includes legal observance, but it goes beyond the legal sphere: Morality cannot be legislated.

6. Life-serving Every person can serve life. For the celibate and unmarried, human sexuality may find expression in a life of dedicated service to people through church or society. For the married, this purpose will generally be realized, not only through service to others, but through the procreation of children.[30] The value of bearing children is presently under heavy attack in a world that stresses full sexual expression and recommends abortion as a medical safety valve.

7. Joyous Wholesome sexual expression should give witness to exuberant appreciation of the gift of life and the mystery of love. It must never become a burden, a merely passive duty, or a heartless conformity to expectation and routine. We should not speak of a "conjugal debt" when speaking of marital relations.

B. Comment on the Criteria of the CTSA Report

According to the authors of *Human Sexuality,* where the above-mentioned values prevail one can be reasonably sure that the sexual behavior involved is wholesome and moral. Conversely, where sexual conduct becomes personally frustrating and self-destructive, manipulative and enslaving, deceitful and dishonest, inconsistent and unstable, indiscriminate and promiscuous, irresponsible and non-life serving, burdensome and repugnant, ungenerous and un-Christlike, it is clear that there is an abuse of the moral order involved.

All of the aforementioned values are empty, however, unless enlightened by the core principle of Christian conduct, the Gospel law of love. This unique dimension of Christian morality must be present in the course of activity and in the pursuit of values.[31]

But is it enough to have this intention? Are there not actions that are good or evil in and of themselves? The criteria presented by the CTSA report fail to address this question.

C. The Levels of Moral Evaluation

In judging moral behavior in general and sexual behavior in particular we are guided by several levels of evaluative criteria.

1. The level of universal principle The ultimate commandment of Christ regarding love of God and love of neighbor is the universal principle of moral behavior. When applying this commandment to sexual behavior, we judge how best to love our neighbor by considering the situation and need of the persons involved. We cannot know in advance the best way of expressing love in a given circumstance. Our specific responsibility and opportunity will unfold in time.

2. The level of particular value Particular values specify the meaning of basic principles. The values related to sexual conduct that have been mentioned in this chapter are not meant to be a checklist but signs of authentic human behavior.

3. The level of concrete norms, rules, and precepts Particular formulations distill from the Christian community the most practical and effective ways that the desired values may be realized in the world. They are meant to enlighten conscience. They should indicate what Christian experience has proven. As such, they are normative, but not universal moral absolutes.

4. The level of decision This is the sphere of personal conscience. The moral guidelines that we have are intended to serve or enlighten conscience; they cannot replace it. The well-informed and well-formed conscience, responsive to principles, guidelines, and values, remains the ultimate subjective norm for evaluating the morality of particular sexual expressions and behavior.

QUESTIONS FOR DISCUSSION

1. Discuss the elements involved in making a decision: opinions, feelings, facts, rules. Relate these to a specific situation, e.g., deciding whether or not to serve in the military.

2. Does the need to respect the uniqueness of the individual necessarily lead to "everybody doing his or her own thing"? Discuss.

3. Saint Augustine once said, "Love and do what you will." Evaluate this statement in terms of personal conscience.

4

The Emerging Woman
of Today

No contemporary book on human sexuality would be complete without a section dedicated to the mystery of woman. Both within and outside the Roman Catholic Church there is much that must be learned about the identity and role of women. For that reason we address ourselves now to the theme of the emerging woman of today.

I. The Witness of Sacred Scripture

We begin our investigation by searching sacred scripture to discover the portrait of woman painted by the sacred authors. Is their view of woman positive or negative? Are we faced with one portrait or many?

A. The Old Testament

The treatment of sex in the Old Testament was influenced both by the demand for cultic purity and by attitudes associated with the patriarchal form of marriage and family. Though women were included in some genealogies (Genesis 4), descent was generally traced from the lineage of the father. As head of the household, the father was usually the one who arranged marriages for his children, even to the point of selecting a wife for his son. The bride was merely a passive spectator whose own father gave her away for a price (Genesis 24:4).

The attitude behind this tradition was also expressed by keeping women in an inferior legal and social position, as though they were property (Exodus 20:7; Jeremiah 6:12).[1] The second and third chapters of Genesis, however, break free from this restricted view to describe the original condition of woman as one of relative equality.[2]

We must note, then, that more than one view of woman is expressed by the authors of sacred scripture. It is especially interesting to look at the book of Deuteronomy which offers a surprisingly positive approach that elevates the legal status of women.[3]

Fundamental to the patriarchal society of the Old Testament, and in accord with the generally inferior position of women, was the functional character given to marriage. The social purpose of marriage in Israel, as in other societies of the time, was not so much the legitimation of sexual intercourse as the procreation of children. In Israel's agricultural society a large family meant a large working force to tend the fields. The need to bear children was so crucial that a sterile wife often supplied her husband with a concubine (Genesis 30:1-13).[4]

Men were given great latitude regarding sexual relations, so long as they respected the rights of their countrymen to a clear line of inheritance. Women, however, were bound to total and unconditional fidelity. They were not permitted to engage in extramarital relations. Thus the understanding of adultery from an Old Testament perspective is an interesting one.[5]

We note here the phenomenon of levirite marriages (Deuteronomy 25:5-10). If a man died without leaving a male heir, his brother was bound to marry the widow and try to have a son who would bear the dead man's name. The main consideration was the preservation of the homogeneity of the family group.

By way of summary, we may say that the Old Testament view of woman ranged from regarding her as chattel or an object of disdain to the affirmation of personhood. Women function in the biblical narratives in a variety of ways. Their roles range from those of leaders, prophets, and judges to mere sex objects.

B. The New Testament

To see adequately the New Testament vision of woman, we must look first to the person and message of Jesus and then to the New Testament kerygma.

1. Jesus   Jesus championed the cause of the oppressed and the despised (Mark 2:15; 3:10-11; John 8:1-11). It is within this context that his affirmative attitude toward women can best be understood.[6] Jesus openly associated with women (Luke 8:2), took compassion on them (Mark 1:29-31; Luke 7:11-19), spoke of them in his parables (Matthew 13:33; Luke 15:8), and counted them among his intimate friends (John 11). He showed little trace of the common ancient assumption that women were inferior. While no single statement of Jesus can be taken as definitive in this respect, his behavior spoke louder than any words in affirming the equality of women.[7]

Awareness of Jesus' concern for the oppressed can help us see more clearly his stand on divorce. His statement on divorce is one of Jesus' most distinctive moral teachings, one that we can ascribe to him personally (Mark 10:2-12; Matthew 5:31-32; 19:3-9). The rabbis had argued for years over what exactly constituted adequate grounds for divorce.[8] Jesus interpreted the law in terms of its purpose, which, indirectly at least, was to circumscribe the arbitrariness of a husband and protect his wife. By demanding grounds for divorce and observance of an orderly process, the law prevented a husband from divorcing his wife through caprice. The prohibition of Jesus on divorce was meant to protect women from male exploitation. He forbade treating women as chattel, disposing of them at will, and leaving them without financial support. Instead he regarded them as partners in marriage.[9]

The whole ministry of Jesus can be characterized as an exercise in divine compassion.[10] For both rabbinic Judaism and the New Testament church, there was to be no distinction between male and female before God (see, for example, Galations 3:28). Jesus was able to break through the androcentric double standard of his society. Jesus required the same faith from both men and women. He placed them both equally under the law of love. As a result, the double standard was shattered. And so, while Jesus did not *per se* proclaim a new sexual ethic, his law of love does have great implications as a universal ethical principle.

2. The New Testament Church The New Testament community accepted the revolutionary attitude of Jesus toward women, at least in theory. Women were called "co-heirs" in the life of grace, according to I Peter 3:7. Saint Paul's affirmation in Galations 3:28 that there is no difference between male and female is the clearest statement of the equal dignity of man and woman in the entire New Testament.[11] What is more, women took an active role in the life of the New Testament community, rendering practical assistance (Acts 9:36), instructing (Acts 18:26), and exercising leadership (Romans 16:1).

Social custom, however, militated against the original feminist impulse in Christianity, and the revolutionary personalism of Jesus toward women was gradually submerged.[12] Silence and submission came to be imposed on women (I Corinthians 14:34). Marriage in the first century was too patriarchal to allow for any other outcome. With the elevation of marriage to a symbol of Christ and the church, the socio cultural status of women became canonized as an idea, a state of affairs sanctioned by the divine will. Women were to be honored, but only as the "weaker" sex.

II. LATER APPROACHES TO WOMAN

A. The Classic Stereotype

In the history of Christian reflection there have been various approaches to sexuality in general that can be termed "inadequate." Probably the most inadequate of these was the position that sexuality is essentially evil. It was part and parcel of this position to define woman as evil, as the source of human sin.

Gnosticism, which gave rise to this idea, was basically a dualistic philosophy in which realities such as spirit, rationality, and logic were seen as good, while matter and emotion were seen as evil. According to Gnosticism's dualistic model, masculinity was good, but femininity was evil. The classic stereotype of woman as more carnal, more emotional, and less logical than man was inherent in this outlook.[13]

B. The Patristic and Scholastic Era

The theme of woman as evil also emerged in the writings of some of the Fathers of the Church. Tertullian called women "the devil's gateway."[14] Saint Jerome wrote passages in which he suggests that women should not wash themselves, because this might increase their seductive potential.[15] Saint Augustine stated that nothing so "debases" a man as does the fondling of a woman.[16] But this particular theme does not totally describe the patristic outlook which contained many positive elements.

When we look at the thought of the Scholastics we continue to see this pessimistic strain. While Saint Thomas Aquinas held that women had souls, he followed Aristotle's idea that female souls were basically "defective" male souls.[17] Up until the time of Saint Albert the Great and Saint Thomas, it was popularly held that the human soul was infused by God forty days after conception in the case of males, but only after eighty days in the case of females.[18]

C. The Shifting Cultural Images of Woman

Besides these thematic views, various cultural images of woman have emerged in the western world.

Two approaches to sexuality that overstress physicality have existed in a variety of shapes and forms over the centuries. These are procreationism, which tends to see women as machines that bear children, and physical sensualism which sees women as objects of the sexual impulses of males.

These two approaches were fostered by the double standard of morality. The double standard barred intercourse outside of marriage for females in order to guarantee a husband that all the children his wife bore were surely his. The double standard did not exclude intercourse outside marriage for males, however, because it was held that males had the right to the physical pleasure available from unmarried women's bodies.[19]

The Roman Catholic Church never officially approved of a double standard of morality, but prominent Christian leaders of past centuries sometimes helped promote the idea that women were physical beings who were less than fully human.[20]

The overly-romantic conception of sexuality that began especially with the troubadours led to another equally inadequate view of woman, a view that held woman in great awe. This position is often called pedestalism, because it puts women on a pedestal where they are praised, while being exempted from much of the wear and tear of daily life.[21] It can be noted that many aspects of Marian devotion in recent centuries have served to reinforce a pedestal-view of woman. While it is necessary and desirable for the church to give appropriate honor to Mary, such devotion needs to be revitalized and depedestalized.[22]

Another cultural phenomenon affecting the position of women has been the taking of stands on particular rights of women. Inequitable laws concerning marriage and divorce, denial of voting rights until very recently, exclusion from certain educational and professional fields are major examples of ways in which society's narrow conception of the meaning of sexuality has worked against women.[23]

III. CURRENT DIFFICULTIES OF WOMEN

The difficulties that women have faced are not just a phenomenon of the past. Various areas in our contemporary life reveal the continuing difficulties of women.

A. Sexism

One contemporary issue is the problem of language. By consistently using male words to refer to both men and women, our language subtly reinforces the notion that women are inferior to men. This may seem like much ado about nothing, and sometimes this may be the case, but it is important to realize that our way of speaking conditions our thinking more than we realize.[24]

On the physical level, women are still treated in our society as sexual objects intended for the pleasure of males. One example of this is pornography; another is advertising. We might also include here prostitution and sexual harassment.[25]

B. The Question of Ministry

The various Christian churches are, at the present time, in a period of declining prestige and credibility within our society. For these church communities to recognize and encourage the many gifts of women would contribute significantly to the revitalization they so desperately need.

This is especially true in the Roman Catholic Church. For centuries, through its institutionalization of the religious life, the church has admitted that other roles for women besides marriage are distinct and necessary possibilities. Increasingly in the church today female leadership is coming not only from these religious women but from lay women as well. Some may assume that any woman, religious or lay, who is interested in ministry is a frustrated seeker of priestly ordination. This is not so. By encouraging the ministry of women in all its forms the church can take an important step toward declericalizing the hierarchy.

When we consider the question of ordination of women in the Roman Catholic Church, it is apparent that, from a strictly theological point of view, most of the arguments against it have lost their strength. I would say, however, that three major factors support the ordination of women.

First, a better developed scriptural hermeneutic has helped us see the weakness of the argument that women should not be ordained because Jesus ordained only men.

Second, since the difference between the sexes is one of kind and not of degree, exclusion of one sex from ordination is not justified on these grounds.

Third, the life of the church would be enriched by the ordination of women.

From a sociological point of view, however, not every culture recognizes the leadership potential of women. Since the church as an institution makes decisions to be applied throughout the world rather than particular cultural groups, it seems that any movement for the ordination of women will not succeed at the present time.[26]

IV. THEOLOGICAL ANTHROPOLOGY OF MALE/FEMALE RELATIONS

Our previous reflections lead to the following question: What is the theology of sexuality and sexual equality? Our study offers a preliminary response to this question by viewing man and woman as full partners in a common humanity. Women are human persons, fully equal to men. But this does not mean men and women are exactly the same.

Our current stress on sexual equality might tempt us to restrict recognition of differences between the sexes to those indisputably evident on the biological/physiological/genetic level.[27] But in the evolution of human thought, human beings have come to view themselves as body-persons, i.e., persons who are a body/soul unity rather than disincarnate spirits who happen to have bodies.[28] Wherever human thought has too radically separated body from soul, poor theories of humanity have resulted.[29] If we accept ourselves as body-persons, we must admit that the tight linkage between our bodies and our spirits has implications for the kinds of persons we are. This does not mean that bodily differences are totally determinative of who we are as human persons. Neither women nor men, for example, should be excluded from a particular vocation or profession on the basis of sex alone, except, of course, in those cases where physical qualifications are a determining factor.[30]

Biological differences between the sexes do have an impact on human personality, however, and these differences are clearly experienced on the level of human relationship. Women have one sort of consciousness in their relationships with men, and another in their relationships with women, just as men have a different kind of consciousness in relating to women than they do in relating to men. It can be noted that this difference in relational consciousness, which is a fundamental anthropological factor of human coexistence, is experienced in all human relationships, not simply in those which include physical or genital expression.[31]

At base, this difference in relational consciousness is a call to all women and men to love others. To love other persons different from ourselves is probably the most fundamental challenge in all of human living. For this reason any so-called unisex theory must be rejected as a form of imprisonment that prevents a person from experiencing the richness and variety of life.

QUESTIONS FOR DISCUSSION

1. Discuss the various scriptural views of woman. Is there any one view that seems more acceptable to you?

2. What is your reaction to the idea of Jesus as a champion of women's rights vis-a-vis the cultural world of his day?

3. Discuss the question of the ordination of women, giving due consideration to historical and sociological data.

5

A Historical Look at Contraception

This chapter traces the development of the Roman Catholic Church's attitudes regarding contraception. As with the evolution of every doctrine, the history of the Christian prohibition against contraception is characterized, not by universal agreement, but by conflict, variety, and personal decision.[1] Although we cannot offer an exhaustive historical analysis we will give a systematic overview to facilitate study and discussion, and to situate better our later presentations on marital sexuality.

I. SHAPING OF THE VISION (50-450)

The roots of the church's attitudes toward contraception extend back to the worlds in which the Christian people had their beginnings.

A. The Jewish World

It is commonly held by scholars that the most common method of birth regulation in the Semitic world was *coitus interruptus.* The Jewish people, as a Semitic group, were familiar with this activity. Besides this practice, other methods of contraception included sterilizing potions, physical objects, and surgery. All of this suggests a knowledge and toleration of birth regulation in the Semitic world.[2]

B. Graeco-Roman World

Among classical writers, potions are the first and most often mentioned form of contraception. Two other common methods

44

were blocking the entrance of the sperm to the uterus and using spermicidal ointments on the male genitals.[3] Besides these mechanical and chemical approaches, a rudimentary knowledge of the female sterile period was employed.

Actual testimony concerning the use of contraceptives is hard to find. Most of the ancient writers did not speak of any moral objection to the dissemination of contraceptive information. The famous Hippocratic Oath, for example, rejected the use of some forms of abortion, but did not discourage contraception.[4]

Throughout the life of the Roman Empire, physicians evidently could obtain contraceptive information easily, but it is a matter of conjecture how widely this information was disseminated. The general impression seems to be that the rich had access to such information while the poor were left to devise their own approaches in this regard.[5]

C. Sacred Scripture

In addition to being influenced by surrounding cultures, early Christianity was guided more directly by the testimony of scripture.

1. Old Testament   The Old Testament contains no condemnation of contraception *per se*. There is no commandment against contraception in any of the legal codes.[6] Thus it is important to note that the alleged traditional condemnation of contraception has no explicit biblical foundation.

It is well-known that the Old Testament strongly favors procreation to the point of tolerating polygamy, concubinage, and even incest so as to perpetuate the species. Yet, there is probably no reputable exegete today who would claim that contraception is condemned in any given biblical text. On the contrary, while the classical incident of Onan (Genesis 38) shows that a nonprocreative use of the seed was at least known, the very silence concerning this practice in the minute and detailed conjugal prescriptions in Deuteronomy and Leviticus indicates that there was some tolerance in this regard.[7]

2. New Testament   The existence of contraceptive methods in the world from which the Christians came is established by the Old Testament, by the Talmud, by Pliny and Aristotle, and by physicians of the Roman Empire. From the prevalence of brutal forms of population control, from fragmentary indications of population decline, and from imperial interest in large families among the rich, we may draw the inference that contraception was a social phenomenon that must have been known to the early Christian community.

In the New Testament marriage is presented as good, and sexual intercourse is presented as holy (see I Thessalonians 4:4). This view is not limited to intercourse for purposes of procreation, for although procreation was held as a value, it was not emphasized as the primary purpose of marriage. Contraception was not expressly treated.

The texts of the New Testament on marriage must be understood in terms of the teaching on virginity.[8] It is this teaching on virginity that marked a break from the Old Testament. The Gospel writers present Jesus himself as being endowed with a holiness that not only excluded sin but also marriage.[9]

Even for Saint Paul intercourse is, at least, lawful for a Christian (I Corinthians 7), and is to be distinguished from a variety of sexual acts that are considered sinful.[10] The holiness found in marital intercourse is sharply distinguished by Paul from sexual behavior that is against nature (see Romans 1:24-27). A few exegetes have contended that the exchange of "natural use" for "unnatural" in this text is intended to rule out anal intercourse within marriage. If this is true, Saint Paul's sentence becomes the most specific New Testament text on a particular form of contraceptive conduct. The prevailing exegesis, however, is that Saint Paul is using the term "unnatural" in a hellenic and stoic sense. "Nature" refers to an intention, a purpose, an order for man discoverable in the universe. It is not identical with each and every impulse expressed by the human person (see Romans 7:15). What is "natural" is not what just occurs spontaneously, but what the human constitution requires.[11]

The use of nature as a standard is not unconnected with a common distrust of magic and drugs associated with magic (see Galations 5:20). But one cannot tell from the various condemnations of *pharmakeia* in the New Testament whether certain drugs only were condemned, or all drugs including contraceptive potions.[12]

D. Stoicism

The teaching of early Christianity on contraception sprang from a combination of doctrinal elements. This doctrinal development, however, was not urged forward primarily by intellectual considerations. Rather it was a response by the Christian community to the pressures of the environment reflected upon in the light of scripture.[13] The shape taken by the teaching depended not only on scripture and thought congenial to Christianity, but also upon forces alien to Christianity.

The prevailing school of thought at the rise of Christianity was Stoicism. The Stoics sought to control bodily desires by means of reason to the point where a person would be rationally self-sufficient and independent of all external forces. During the first three centuries Christian moralists were attracted to the Stoic distruct of pleasure and stress on procreative purpose. They shared the Stoic belief that sexual activity ought to serve not love but nature.[14]

Stoic thought implicity excluded contraception on grounds of family pride and civic responsibility.

E. Gnosticism and Paganism

The formation of an early Christian doctrine on contraception can be seen basically as a response to Gnosticism, which was hostile to procreation, and Paganism, which was indifferent to the sanctity of life.

Gnosticism, of itself, admitted to various strains of development. It was a special mixture of Christian theology and sexual morality.[15] The Gnostic vision de-emphasized marriage and its relation to children. Intercourse was valued as an experience in itself with no necessary connection to procreation as a justifying purpose.

Christianity responded to Gnosticism by turning to the Old Testament, the New Testament, and the law of nature. This last source proved to be most interesting. The church turned to nature as a source of value. If an act was perceived to be natural, it was, therefore, good. The "natural" was distinguished from the "unnatural." Procreation was natural and, hence, good.[16]

We note some of the thoughts of leading Fathers in this regard. Saint John Chrysostom maintained that the generative act is sacred and should not be tampered with. Any interference could be considered an attack on God, and thus contraception would be a mutilation of nature.[17] Saint Ambrose held that a generative purpose is a bare excuse for intercourse when generation is possible, but such sexual activity is only tolerable and not to be encouraged. Intercourse for the old or pregnant would not only be shameful, but also "unnatural," because generation would not be possible.[18] Saint Jerome stated that the act of intercourse is lustful unless used for the purpose of procreation.[19]

Given the pagan disregard for life in the Graeco-Roman world, the church recognized an obligation to defend the sanctity of life. Contraception was seen as an attack on life, but actual statements condemning contraception were relatively few at this point. They may be found in the *Didache,* the *Epistle of Barnabas,* and the *Octavius* of Minucius Felix.[20]

F. The Manichees and Saint Augustine

Manichaeanism was both a theological explanation of the world and a plan of conduct for society. From the sexual point of view, the Manichees separated intercourse from procreation and, in fact, opposed procreation. They praised intercourse with non-ejaculation, because this was intentionally nonprocreative.

It is necessary to understand Manichaeanism in order to appreciate properly the attitude of Saint Augustine regarding contraception. Perhaps of some influence as well was his guilt over his own youthful sexual activity. So far as Augustine was concerned, intercourse was justified only by its relation to procreation; thus marital intercourse was good. Saint Augustine, however, saw nothing spiritual, rational, or sacramental in the act of intercourse itself.[21]

Saint Augustine spoke of the goods of marriage as offspring, fidelity, and stability.[22] By offspring he meant not just physical multiplication of human beings but the generation of new members for Christ. By fidelity he meant the rendering of the marital "debt" to enable the partners to avoid illicit intercourse and ease the flame of carnal desire. By stability he meant that marriage was to be an indissoluble union.

Saint Augustine valued continence above procreation, because procreation had to be rejected in order to reach continence. Continence, however, was not a higher good than fidelity, because fidelity was a virtue that had its source in God, while continence was more a question of will power. Within Augustine's framework only sexual intercourse for the purpose of procreation could be legitimate. So, while marriage was seen as good, the carnal desire involved tinged the good of intercourse with evil.[23]

Thus both the Manichees and Saint Augustine shared a suspicion of sexuality. For the Manichees the ideal would be virginity. For Saint Augustine, the procreative purpose makes the sexual act good even though it contains an element of lust.[24] From his writings, one can infer that Saint Augustine intended to condemn individual acts of contraception. He was opposed to the Manichaean approval of *coitus interruptus.*

II. THE CONDEMNATION (450-1450)

In the period known as the Dark Ages attitudes toward contraception became specified and standardized in the form of laws and prohibitions.

A. The Monastic Contribution

During this period the monks served as the beacons of culture and civilization. The monastic experience of uniformity led to the development of a sexual ethic that was both rigorous and pessimistic. This ethic would later take the form of a code for behavior.[25] Within this ethic contraception was the central problem that had to be faced, because it was considered as homicide in an age when sexual activity with no procreative intent had resulted in a low birth rate.

Several persons formed a corporate opposition to contraception. According to Caesarius of Arles and Martin of Braga (circa 503-543), the sole purpose of marital intercourse was procreation. Without this intention, intercourse would be venially sinful *per se*. They were both especially opposed to magical means of contraception such as roots, herbs, and potions, since these were espoused by the Manichees in their opposition to procreation.

In Rome no explicit teaching on contraception appeared. But authoritative support was given, especially in the thought of Pope Saint Gregory the Great, to a new doctrine on marital intercourse that was very severe. The *Pastoral Rule* of Saint Gregory maintained that pleasure was an unlawful purpose in intercourse. If pleasure were to be mixed with the act of intercourse, then venial sin would be committed.[26] I would see this *Pastoral Rule* as an extreme adaptation of the stoic mistrust of pleasure within which contraception would appear as a monstrous denial of the single excuse for coitus.

B. The Penitential Books

During this time period moral guide books were written for confessors to assist them in assigning penances. These penitential books provided a listing of sins with appropriate penances or tariffs for each.

References to contraception in these books can be found no earlier than the eighth century. Contraceptive actions were always

49

considered serious sins and treated with the utmost severity. In fact, the drinking of a contraceptive potion was considered homicide. We note the words of Regino of Prum:

> If someone (*si aliquis*), to satisfy his lust, or in deliberate hatred, does something to a man or woman so that no children be born of him or her, or gives them to drink, so that he cannot guarantee generation, or her, conception, let it be held as homicide.[27]

This particular paragraph from the penitential books was preserved in the law of the church until the 1917 revision of Canon Law.

In 1230 Saint Raymond of Penafort, under the direction of Pope Gregory IX, compiled the *Decretals*. The *Decretals* incorporated *si aliquis* into its code and what emerged was a papally sponsored law for the entire church that universally opposed contraception in an official way.[28] The *Decretals* were opposed to the use of artificial means of contraception, but not all nonprocreative intercourse came under condemnation.

C. The Cathars

At this time there emerged within the church a new group known as the Cathars. Their ideology was not opposed to marriage, but to procreation. Influenced by the code of courtly love of the troubadours, they praised the love of man for woman, separated love from marriage, celebrated sexual pleasure, and rejected procreative intention, all under the theme of pure love.[29] It seems to me that this pure love could actually be reduced to carnal love in which extramarital intercourse would be the final moment. This thought of the troubadours allowed the idea of sexual affectivity, overlooked by orthodox theology, to surface.

D. Scholasticism

From 1275-1300, the connection between procreation and intercourse was again asserted. Procreation was seen as good—the very reason for intercourse.

The role of pleasure in intercourse seems to have been overlooked for the most part. Thus contraception was not only condemned by the *Decretals,* but excluded by this view of marriage. The common practice of the Scholastic writers was to identify artificial contraceptives under the comprehensive but blind phrase, "poisons of sterility."[30] They saw no moral difference between temporary or permanent sterility.

In the 13th century a list of marital sins came to the fore. *Coitus interruptus,* oral intercourse, anal intercourse, and departure from the standard male-dominant position were considered against nature.[31] This list, however, was prepared to guide individual conscience, and was not widely and publicly enforced.

At this point, then, we find reaffirmation of the condemnation of contraception based on the argument from authority, the thinking of the Fathers of the Church, and the *Decretals.* No biblical texts, no encyclicals, and no conciliar statements supported the condemnation.

The view that contraception is homicide, although indicated in the thought of Saint Augustine and the penitential books, was not a dominant theological tradition. Rather, contraception was commonly condemned as a sin against nature.[32] Other sins against nature included masturbation, bestiality, and sodomy.

According to the dominant theological vision of the time, nature protected the inseminating function by special postures such as the male-dominant position. Any violation of this posture would be in opposition to nature's plan. According to Saint Thomas Aquinas, the marital act itself has been imbued with a God-given quality that should not be touched by rational control.[33] Any interference with the process could be considered a direct assault upon God, thus giving the act itself the absolute value of God. According to the followers of Saint Thomas, the biological function of the sexual act is given by God and cannot be altered by persons.

The followers of Saint Thomas arrived at a synthesis on this question. For them the norm is heterosexual marital coitus performed in the male-dominant position and resulting in insemination. This norm is ordained by God and any departure from this can be considered as a direct offense against God. Thus contraception has to be condemned because it blocks the free and conscious procreative purpose of the couple.[34] According to Saint Augustine, in a previous century, it is this procreative purpose that frees marital intercourse from sin. Accordingly, the use of contraception destroys potential life and destroys the inseminating purpose of intercourse.

During this time no Catholic practicing contraception could consider himself/herself in the state of grace and he or she was barred from receiving the sacraments. Within the sacramental experience of penance, contraception was treated as a private sin, and the penitent was encouraged to fast, pray, mortify the senses, and perform good works.

E. Counter-approaches

Some counter-approaches to this dominant stand appeared between the years 1150 and 1450. While a small number of medieval theologians stressed limitless procreation in order to increase the number of souls born for Christ, the majority promoted the ideal of virginity.

By this time celibacy was the established norm for the clergy in the West. This state was considered to be one of spiritual superiority. Within such a perspective, large families were to be discouraged, since the spiritual and physical welfare of children was seen as a greater value than unlimited procreation.[35] It was considered better not to bear a child than to bear a child who would not have the basic opportunities for education and welfare.[36] The metaphysical principle, "It is better to be than not to be," was not applied here.[37]

According to Saint Thomas, the sacramental good of marriage pertains not to the use of matrimony, but to its essence. In other words, sexual intercourse does not have a sacramental value, and sexual pleasure is not of itself a human act. But since matrimonial coitus is good, so must the pleasure involved be good. In this light, Richard Middleton (1272) maintained the value of moderate pleasure, in other words, pleasure governed by temperance.[38]

During this period, several conscious methods of avoiding conception were seen not to be contraceptive. These means were *coitus reservatus* (periodic abstinence), *amplexus reservatus* (penetration and non-ejaculation), and *coitus interruptus* (withdrawal before ejaculation, ejaculation outside the vagina).

III. INNOVATIONS AND PRESERVATION OF THE RULE (1450-1750)

In the course of the next 300 years voices began to speak out in favor of sexual intercourse as an expression of love and a source of legitimate pleasure.

A. New Insights Regarding Purpose of Intercourse

In the thought of Martin LeMaistre we come across the term conjugal chastity which describes a mid-point between immodesty and insensitivity. In an attempt to legitimate the nonprocreative purpose of marriage, LeMaistre held that pleasure may be sought, because it is associated with an honest end.[39] John Major developed this thought by maintaining that marriage was meant not only to produce offspring, but also to provide consolation and mutual service.[40]

What is important to note here is the shift in approach or method. Prior to this time moralists following the Stoic-Augustinian approach had reflected upon animal experience and then applied their conclusions to human beings. The new method involved looking at the experience of Christian couples. Moralists following this approach concluded that pleasure, in and of itself, is neither right nor wrong, since it follows upon action and it is only willed action that is either moral or immoral. The great commentator on the thought of Saint Thomas Aquinas, Thomas del vio Cajetan, held that a non-precreative use of marriage could be lawful if it was intended as an alternative for fornication.[41]

The 16th century was an age of transition inspired by the great theological controversies over grace, concupiscence, and original sin. One of the leading figures during this time was Thomas Sanchez, S.J. (1550-1610). For Sanchez the touchstone of marital morality was the experience of the Christian couple who sought to love God. In defending the sexual contact of spouses apart from coitus, he sought to establish love as a value apart from procreation.[42] Through the thought of Sanchez we see that marital coitus was no longer necessarily viewed as being definitively procreative. In other words, procreation could be mentally excluded from acts of intercourse.

During the 16th century theologians began to see the fulfillment of human needs such as material welfare and education as taking precedence over the right to marital intercourse. As regards methods of avoiding conception other than abstinence, some said that *amplexus reservatus* was legitimate while others said that it was not. The negative viewpoint was based on the biological thought of the first century Roman physician Galen who maintained the presence of a female seed that was discharged with orgasm.[43]

By way of summary, we note a rejection of the Augustinian view that intercourse may be initiated only for the purpose of procreation. A number of values associated with intercourse, ranging from health to pleasure, were defended. Love had been introduced as a value, yet, the prohibition against contraception remained firm.

B. A Stronger Defensive Position

Until the 19th century no important group urged the control of birth. The standard reason approved by moralists for refusing marital intercourse or practicing *amplexus reservatus* was the factor of oppressive poverty. This was a key insight, namely that the procreation of children could be limited for a socio-economic reason.

In an effort to avoid large families, the poor, the middle class, and the nobility adopted one of the possible alternatives to contraception—continence, *amplexus reservatus,* or the postponement of marriage. Since these measures were not entirely satisfactory, modification of the doctrine was sought. Efforts in this regard, however, were never translated into official doctrinal change.

Why was this the case? Institutional involvement by the church was lacking; the medical field was not publicly represented; and technically improved methods of birth control did not exist. The only development in this regard was the introduction of the condom in the mid-17th century.[44] Added to these factors was a social environment that opposed change, Protestant rigidity concerning all sexual matters, and the fact that all sins associated with sex were considered equally evil.

Hence the rules against contraception remained without modification. The church's position shaped in reaction to Gnostic, Manichaean, and Cathar repudiation of procreativity, now had no dialectical opposite. A defensive stance was assumed and supportive arguments for the opposition to contraception began to develop. The *Roman Catechism* and the Papal Bull *Effraenatum* of Pope Sixtus V viewed contraception as homicide.[45] According to this approach the giving or taking of contraceptives was to be treated literally as murder in terms of canon law and state law. This legislation was repealed in 1590 by Pope Gregory XIV.[46] It is interesting to note that Saint Alphonsus Liguori did not liken contraception to homicide.[47]

The most direct argument used against contraception was the fact that the vagina is the natural and appropriate vessel created to receive the male seed. This ruled out oral sex, anal sex, and *coitus interruptus.* During this time the church seemingly made no strong effort to communicate to the faithful any doctrine on contraception. The differences between the earlier opinion so strenuously proposed, and the new position taken by Sanchez, LeMaistre, and, to some extent, Saint Alphonsus, was measurable.

Although the sanctions in regard to contraception were better organized in the 17th century than in the 13th century, they were softened by the principles of invincible ignorance and cooperation developed by Saint Alphonsus Liguori in his *Theologia Moralis.* More people were informed of their marital duties as a result of education and spiritual reading.

By the mid-18th century the stringent teaching of Canon Law and the *Roman Catechism* had been diluted. Contraception was no longer viewed as homicide, but as a violation of the purpose of marriage.[48] The tendency was to move away from the rigors of the medieval position. Without a doubt, contraception was still condemned, but the grounds for its condemnation were weakening.

IV. FURTHER DEVELOPMENTS AND CONTROVERSY (1750-1965)

A. The Socio-cultural Climate

The end of the 18th century was marked by the decline of the birth rate in Europe and the open advocacy of birth control as a socially acceptable practice. With the advent of the new rationalism, nature and human persons were regarded as machines that could be perfected and controlled. Social, political, moral, and economic considerations promoted growing opposition to uncontrolled procreation.[49] As a result, in the first half of the 19th century individual decisions to limit births became increasingly common. The clergy approached the Roman Congregations asking them to pass judgment on questions concerning birth control.

Unfortunately, the church at that time was confined in the intellectual shell of an impoverished Scholasticism. No intellectual giants came forward to relate the rich heritage of the church's past to the neo-intellectual spirit that had emerged. Moral theologians, because they were not scientifically grounded, were especially weak and characterized by timidity, convention, and prudery.[50] Only the tolerant pastoral vision of Saint Alphonsus Liguori relieved the intellectual torpor. It is against this background that the first Roman responses to birth control must be seen.

B. Theological/Canonical Questions

These early questions concerned two practical issues, namely the responsibility of the spouse who cooperated in contraception, and the responsibility of the confessor to inquire about the sin.

1. Cooperation Between 1816 and 1823 three statements were made by the Sacred Penitentiary, the Roman Tribunal for matters pertaining to the sacrament of penance. On November 15, 1816 the Penitentiary stated that if by refusing her husband a woman would be badly treated or harmed by him, she might have intercourse although she knew from experience that her husband would withdraw and ejaculate outside her vagina.[51] On April 23, 1822 the Penitentiary stated that if a man threatened to leave his wife or beat her if she refused, she could have intercourse with him even if she knew he intended to ejaculate outside the vagina. This opinion was also repeated on February 1, 1823.[52] On April 19, 1853 the Holy Office stated that a wife was not permitted to submit to intercourse with her husband if he used a condom.[53]

2. Inquiry The thought of Saint Alphonsus Liguori became axiomatic on this issue: "As to sins in marriage, ask the wife if she has paid the marital debt; about other things be silent, unless asked."[54] If any questioning were to be done, it was to be done in a general fashion.

3. Condemnation of Contraception During this period the arguments against contraception were focused on *coitus interruptus,* which was branded as onanism.[55] A vigorous attack on birth control gained prominence only in the last quarter of the 19th century, and was definitively stated in 1930 with the publication of the encyclical *Casti Connubii.*

C. The 20th Century: Protest and Response

As the 20th century progressed a growing body of medical opinion was convincing the general public to accept birth control.[56] The trend reached its apex in 1930 at the *Lambeth Conference* when the Church of England withdrew its absolute prohibition against contraception.[57]

Although Pope Leo XIII issued the encyclical *Arcanum Divinae Sapientiae,* it contained nothing explicit on contraception, but rather concerned itself with the growing phenomenon of divorce.[58] The first strongest papal statement on birth control since *Effraenatum,* therefore, was the 1930 encyclical of Pope Pius XI, *Casti Connubii.* Inspired by the profound moralist Arthur Vermeersch, S.J., the encyclical sought to dispel doubt and uncertainty. It offered a synthesis, but made poor use of history and context. The divine institution of marriage was upheld as well as the goodness of offspring, the latter being seen as the primary good of the marital union.[59] The condemnation of contraception came through loud and clear: *Those who exercising it (i.e. the marital union) deliberately deprive it of its natural force and power (i.e. by contraception), act against nature and effect what is base and indecent.*[60] This view was reinforced by a statement indicating the gravity of the sin, namely that it was a sin against fidelity.[61]

It is evident that the condemnation of *Casti Connubii* was not restricted to *coitus interruptus* and thus the document does have immense doctrinal authority. The encyclical spoke separately on the issue of sterilization.[62] As regards confessional inquiry, Pope Pius XI made it clear that, for the common good, the sinfulness of contraception must be made known to all.[63]

D. The Dispute of Methods

In this century the debate over contraception has centered chiefly on a moral evaluation of various methods. A survey of these methods follows.

1. The Use of the Sterile Period   No theoretical development supported the deliberate use of the sterile period before 1873. The theologian Auguste Lecomte is the first to take account of the 19th century discoveries regarding ovulation. His work was basically a commentary upon the work of Ernst von Baer, the discoverer of the human ovum.[64] He recommended that a couple be allowed to restrict intercourse to the infertile time period as a means of family control.

In 1924 Kyusaku Ogino and in 1929 Hermann Knaus, operating independently, published their findings determining that ovulation occurred sixteen to twelve days before the anticipated first day of the next menstrual period.[65] On October 19, 1951 Pope Pius XII stated that a couple could use the "rhythm method," avoiding intercourse during the woman's fertile period, if there were sufficient reason.[66] For a couple to avoid the duty of procreation by using rhythm without serious reason would be a sin. Thus the rhythm method was finally sanctioned in 1951 after almost twenty years of popularization.

2. *Amplexus Reservatus*   Moralists were divided regarding the morality and practice of this method. In 1951 Hyacinth Hering, O.P. attacked *amplexus reservatus,* calling it a destruction of the ability to generate offspring.[67] On June 30, 1952 the Holy Office issued a *monitum* warning theologians not to urge this method.[68] But Francis Hurth, S.J. took a different stance. According to Hurth, some incomplete genital acts were defensible, but not all were lawful. Some acts, by their natural structure, were evidently in the natural line of sexual activity, and such was his view of this method.[69]

3. Other Means   By the term *copula dimidiata* is meant the partial penetration of the vagina with insemination. Most theologians felt that this method could be used with sufficient reason.[70] Regarding the use of anaphrodisiacs, it was determined that their use in the production of impotency or sterility would be sinful.[71]

4. Sterilizing Operations   *Casti Connubii* had condemned self-mutilation in general, and compulsory sterilization in particular. Pope Pius XII restated this position by maintaining that direct sterilization would be a serious violation of moral law.[72] The literature of moral casuistry had much to say regarding sterilization especially in connection with the concept of double effect and the principle of totality.[73] It became apparent that sterilization presented moral problems distinct from those of *coitus interruptus* or the condom. It was against this background that the controversies over the pill developed.

5. Pills   In the early 1950s the first contraceptive pill for commercial use appeared. This was *hesperidin,* an antienzyme that affected the hyaluronidase present in the semen. Taken orally by both husband and wife for a prescribed period, it was supposed to prevent infecundation of the ovum. What was affected was the generative process itself, thus this was condemned.[74]

In 1953 a progesterone pill was developed which, taken orally by a woman over a period of days, would make conception impossible. This pill acted upon the thalamopituitary complex in such a way as to prevent the secretion of hormones that would cause the ovary to release an ovum.[75] Its effect was comparable to the natural suspension of ovulation during pregnancy due to the secretion of progesterone.

Two other effects, however, emerged as well. The pill seemed to change the physical consistency of the cervical mucus and also affected the endometrium (the mucus membrane lining the uterus). Thus if the pill failed to prevent ovulation, it might still prevent pregnancy either by preventing fecundation (fertilization of the ovum by the sperm) or nidation (attachment of the fertilized ovum to the wall of the uterus). The prevention of nidation was viewed by moralists as abortion, but this position was not proven.[76]

In the theological debates between 1957 and 1964 the pill was regarded solely as an anovulant, i.e. as an agent that prevented conception by preventing ovulation. During this time period no theologian would defend the lawfulness of anovulants in regulating fertility, unless it was a question of correcting the menstrual cycle or regulating lactation.

Then in 1963 *The Time Has Come* by John Rock was 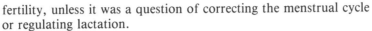 The author argued that the use of anovulants would be

Ovulation was naturally during pregnancy, thus preventing another pregnancy that would harm the already existing fetus; why could not persons inhibit ovulation when a new pregnancy might endanger the education of already existing offspring? This position was rejected by several American theologians including Connell, Ford, Lynch, and Kelly. It was also rejected by Cardinal Cushing of Boston on April 30, 1963.[77]

The debate about the pill continued in the Netherlands under the influence of Louis Janssens and William van der Marck. They maintained that if one had intercourse only at sterile times, one placed a temporal obstacle to procreation. This method of birth control had been accepted by Pope Pius XII on the grounds that the placing of a temporal obstacle was not illicit so long as the structure of the act was respected. Would not the same reasoning apply if one placed an obstacle by means of progesterone pills?[78]

On June 23, 1964, with bishops and theologians divided, Pope Paul VI announced that the church would study the question.[79] The results of this study were announced to the world on July 29, 1968 in the encyclical *Humanae Vitae*. We now turn our attention to that encyclical.

QUESTIONS FOR DISCUSSION

1. How do you understand the term doctrinal development? Use contraception as an example.

2. How do you evaluate the influence of Saint Augustine upon the Christian vision of sexuality?

3. What is your opinion regarding the use of anovulants in the regulation of ovulation?

4. How do you summarize the pros and cons of the rhythm method?

6

An Analysis of the Encyclical Humanae Vitae

The publication of Pope Paul VI's encyclical *Humanae Vitae* on July 29, 1968 touched off events that were unprecedented in recent church history. A large number of theologians all over the world publicly declared they could not give unqualified assent to the encyclical. The publicity given by the mass media heightened the controversy. This papal letter, perhaps more than any other church document in recent times, touched off a debate that continues to this day, a debate that involves clergy and hierarchy, laity and religious, theologians and scientists, both within and outside of the Roman Catholic Church.[1]

While this chapter does not claim to be an exhaustive treatment of the questions raised by the encyclical, it will attempt to illustrate the issues and attitudes, arguments and counter-arguments involved.

I. SHIFT IN THE ECCLESIOLOGICAL VISION

After Vatican I, which had defined the doctrine of papal infallibility, a certain theological tendency emerged which vastly enlarged the claims of the magisterium. This view of hierarchical authority went beyond the strict definitions given in the Dogmatic Constitution *Pastor Aeternus* of Vatican I:

> That the Roman Pontiff, when he speaks *ex cathedra,* that is, when in discharge of his office of pastor and doctor of all Christians, by

virtue of his supreme apostolic authority, he defines a doctrine regarding faith and morals to be held by the universal Church, by the divine assistance promised to him by blessed Peter, is possessed of that divine infallibility with which the Divine Redeemer willed that His Church should be endowed for defining doctrine regarding faith and morals; and that therefore such definitions of the Roman Pontiff are irreformable of themselves and not from the consent of the Church.[2]

While Vatican I restricted papal infallibility to *ex cathedra* pronouncements, there was a tendency within Catholic theological literature to attribute infallibility to the ordinary teaching of the pope or, without going that far, to assign to this teaching such high authority that neither bishops nor theologians were allowed to qualify it. The pope became almost the sole authoritative teacher in the church. Another theological tendency was to enlarge the area of infallibility to include doctrines loosely connected with divine revelation, human wisdom, and rational morality.[3]

Vatican II tried to reverse this trend. While confirming the teaching of Vatican I on papal infallibility and papal primacy in general, it limited infallibility to the sphere of divine revelation. Also, the teaching of the pope was placed within the ecclesial context of the episcopal college.[4]

The publication of *Humanae Vitae* ruptured the ecclesiological vision that was beginning to emerge. The issue of contraception treated in the encyclical had been withdrawn from discussion at Vatican II and removed from the agenda of the Synod of Bishops in 1967. Bypassing this collegial process, the pope instead consulted a Pontifical Commission that had been established by Pope John XXIII. The papal statement that emerged following this consultation was an authoritative teaching framed in the language of Roman neoscholasticism and removed from the plural structures of the thinking community of the universal church.[5]

How then should such an authoritative teaching be received? The assent due to noninfallible teaching is termed religious assent. While this assent involves the objective obedience of mind and heart, it is not an act of faith. Because the statement under consideration is noninfallible and thus could be wrong, the assent is always conditional. In other words, there are conditions under which it is licit for a Catholic to dissent from an official position. To deny the possibility of such dissent would be to presume the infallibility of the document, a claim that was never made for *Humanae Vitae*.[6]

II. THE PAPAL COMMISSION

The Papal Commission consulted by Paul VI represented a large spectrum of opinions, attitudes, and theologies.[7] Ultimately the group submitted two reports to the pope for study.

A. The Minority Report

This report argued that Christian tradition has always assumed some basic truths and has taught them constantly and universally as true. I maintain that this report fails to offer a philosophical analysis of human nature or natural law when speaking of contraception. In fact, the tradition of the church lacks a clear philosophical understanding of human nature.

The contributors noted an uninterrupted continuity in the church's response to the question; "Is contraception always seriously evil?" According to this report, the church has continuously maintained that artificial means of birth control are always and everywhere intrinsically evil, and states:

> The Church cannot change her answer because this answer is true. Whatever may pertain to a more perfect formulation of the teaching or its possible genuine development, the teaching itself cannot be substantially changed. It is true because the Catholic Church, instituted by Christ to show men a secure way to eternal life, could not have so wrongly erred during all these centuries of its history.[8]

The minority report analyzes two central terms, "contraception" and "always evil." Contraception is defined as any use of the marriage right in the exercise of which the act is deprived through human intervention of its natural power for the procreation of life.[9] The expression "always evil" is understood as referring to something that can never be justified by any motive or any circumstance because it is always intrinsically evil; it is wrong, not because of any precept of positive law, but by reason of the natural law.[10]

According to this report, one can find no period in history, no theological school, and scarcely one Catholic theologian who ever denied that contraception was always seriously evil. This report contends that the church has been absolutely constant on this issue. As a result, the report concludes:

> The teaching of the Church did not have its beginning in *Casti Connubii*, nor does it depend on the precise degree of authority with

which Pius XI wished to teach the Church in that document. The teaching of the Church in this matter would have its own validity and truth even if *Casti Connubii* had never been written.[11]

The philosophical foundation of the minority report is the contention that nature is unchanging. This report seems to equate God's way with nature's way and the natural law with the divine law.[12]

In traditional moral theology the law of nature has been viewed as the proximate norm of morality, while the will of God has usually been named as the ultimate norm of action.[13] According to the minority report, a person can, at least indirectly, reach the will of the Creator of nature by discovering this will in the laws of nature. This would be the foundation for an objective moral theology as opposed to moral subjectivism.[14]

By way of objection I must note that it is not exactly the order of nature itself that reveals God's will. Today, human beings do not stand in awe of brute nature as though it were the expression of a divine force. Rather, the challenge to human beings is to discover the will of God by interpreting and directing the movement of nature. This interpretation can lead a person to either an atheistic or a theistic interpretation of life.[15]

Not only do people today not understand the idea that the movement of nature is synonymous with God's will, they reject it. We see ourselves as having a positive and dominating control over nature. Today the human race assumes total responsibility for itself; by work, rationality, and creativity we seek to become fully masters of the universe. Therefore, the starting point in moral decision-making must be anthropological, for it is in human persons and not brute nature that we see God's image and likeness.[16]

When Saint Thomas Aquinas used the phrase "law of nature," he certainly did not intend to refer to pure biology, but rather to the ethical sphere.[17] For him law is a command issued to conscience. It is a general moral sense within the human heart. By the light of conscience we participate in the divine design for the human race.[18]

I would maintain, contrary to the minority report, that natural law is not a complex of principles. Rather, I would hold that natural law, interpreted as God's design for human persons and the world, can be discovered only by the light of reason reflecting on human experience in order to determine the sense, meaning, and purpose of life. Reason does not create its own values, but discovers values by reflecting on the facts of experience.[19]

According to the minority report we can also look at natural law in a certain directed sense. Thus contraceptives and anovulants would be immoral because they interfere with the natural functions for which the sexual organs were intended by the Creator.[20] This seems to me to be an inadequate argument because it fails to take into account any psychology of sexuality and ignores the mystery of interpersonal and intrapersonal relationships.

In opposition to the minority report, I would contend that the sexual impulse must be used for human ends; it cannot be allowed to function in an unplanned manner, for persons are called upon to humanize themselves and their world.

B. The Majority Report

According to the perspective of this report, biology is not the essential determinant in the question of contraception; rather the total, personal context of each situation must be objectively considered. In other words, biological structures in and of themselves are not ethical norms.[21]

In opposition to the ahistorical view of human nature espoused by the members of the minority, the majority report maintains the historicity of humankind, namely that man and woman are continually discovering more and more values in their lives with the aid of the various sciences. Thus the argument of the majority report centers on phenomenological analysis and not on the tradition of the magisterium. While the minority report showed the constant and universal teaching of the church regarding contraception, the majority report studied the values that ought to be realized in a conjugal relationship and asked whether or not contraception always detracted from this realization.[22]

According to the majority report, a harmony must be established among the various elements within a marriage so that contraception will be either neutral or immoral when seen in relation to the other human values present. Thus, according to the majority, one cannot brand every intervention in the generative processes as being intrinsically immoral for, indeed, sometimes such intervention may be necessary and even worthy of praise when the totality of conjugal values is threatened.[23]

A right ordering towards the good of the child within the conjugal and familial community pertains to the essence of human sexuality. Therefore the morality of sexual acts between married people takes its meaning first of all and specifically from the ordering of their actions in a fruitful married life, that is one which is practiced with responsible, generous, and prudent parenthood. It does not then depend upon the direct fecundity of each and every particular act.[24]

In short, the majority attempted to evolve a theology based upon the traditional concept of marriage as a project or process that is lived over the course of a lifetime. In this regard they employed the principle of totality as a governing principle for sexual activity within the marriage context.

III. HUMANAE VITAE

At the very core of this papal encyclical we find a disagreement with the underlying philosophical/theological framework of the majority report and a reaffirmation of the traditional viewpoint on natural law, a view that fundamental biological life-processes are such that we can discover in them certain intentions of the Creator. According to this traditional vision, the two aspects of conjugal love, procreativity and mutuality, can never be separated. As I see it, this is the key to the understanding of the encyclical:

That teaching, often set forth by the Magisterium, is founded upon the inseparable connection, willed by God and unable to be broken by man on his own initiative, between the two meanings of the conjugal act: the unitive meaning and the procreative meaning.[25]

Pope Paul VI is very clear and unambiguous when he forbids all forms of intervention in the procreative process other than the so-called rhythm method.[26] Pope Paul VI argues that the light of reason discovers functions in the human person that he or she must respect in order to conform to the will of the Creator of those same functions.[27]

According to the encyclical, conjugal love as it is expressed in sexual relations, can never be separated from the possibility of procreation. Any attempt at separation, especially through the use of artificial devices, for whatever reason, would be always and everywhere wrong and immoral. Pope Paul VI thus rejects any and all forms of human intervention in the procreation act which have, as their main purpose, the contraceptive use of intercourse.[28] This prohibition would include chemicals, artificial devices, *coitus interruptus,* sterilization, and abortion. Rhythm is permitted because it respects the laws of God inscribed in the generative processes.[29]

From my perspective it seems that the central assertions of the encyclical, "each and every marital act must remain open to the transmission of life," does not deal with the readiness to transmit life.[30] The fact that a couple is not always ready to conceive a child is obvious even on the biological level since a woman is only fertile for a certain number of days during her cycle.

Humanae Vitae confines the procreative meaning of the marital act to the faithful observance of biological laws and rhythms. This implies that God's divine plan is revealed to the spouses through absolutely sacred physiological laws. The basic flaw here lies in the fact that the encyclical declares biological laws to be absolutely binding on conscience.[31] Thus a question emerges: Is a person to be absolutely subjected to biological laws and rhythms or is he or she to be their wise administrator? *Humanae Vitae* responds:

> In fact, just as man does not have unlimited dominion over his body in general, so also, with particular reason, he has no such dominion over his generative faculties as such, because of their intrinsic ordination towards raising up life, of which God is the principle.[32]

And yet, the problem remains. The encyclical equates the sacredness of biological functions and the sacredness of human life. In fact, the personal dimension of the individual is seemingly subordinate to biological function.

Furthermore, Pope Paul VI seems to say that any effort of man and woman to be the stewards of biological reality is arbitrary; persons are expected to be submissive, simply and absolutely, to biological laws and rhythms, at least in the sense that each marital act must be open to the possibility of giving life. Thus for the encyclical, human biology, and not human reason, should determine the fruitfulness or nonfruitfulness of the conjugal act.[33]

I would agree that human persons ought never to act arbitrarily; they must make the best possible use of all the gifts of God; each must administer to his or her biological and psychological heritage in an atmosphere of generous responsibility to self, to others, and to the spouse.

The encyclical proceeds:

> If, then, there are serious motives to space out births, which derive from the physical or psychological conditions of husband and wife, or from external conditions, the Church teaches that it is licit to take into account the natural rhythms immanent in the generative functions, for the use of marriage in the infecund periods only, and in this way to regulate births.[34]

The only solution proposed by *Humanae Vitae* is to bring rhythm to perfect functioning and to let married people determine the infecund days. This frame of reference would suggest a place for a *Catholic pill,* in other words a pill that would ascertain or fix the time of ovulation; such regulation would respect the established order of the Creator and the natural laws and rhythms, while a pill that postponed ovulation would be intrinsically evil and immoral since it did not respect these laws.[35]

It seems logical to wonder why a pill that fixes the date of ovulation and guarantees the loss of the ovule be considered more "Catholic" than a pill that preserves the ovule which, here and now, is not needed because procreation would be irresponsible? *Humanae Vitae* defends its position:

> In defending conjugal morals in their integral wholeness, the Church knows that she contributes towards the establishment of a truly human civilization; she engages man not to abdicate from his own responsibility in order to rely on technical means; by that very fact she defends the dignity of man and wife."[36]

If persons were to rely on technical means alone without discernment in the proper use of these means, I would say that humankind would be degraded. But *Humanae Vitae* contends that the use of any technical means of birth prevention would necessarily destroy the integrity of conjugal love. This point cannot be grounded in experience. It assumes that biological laws and rhythms, if dutifully followed, best protect human dignity and the capacity to love.

IV. THEOLOGICAL REFLECTION

As we have noted throughout this book, sexuality as lived by human persons is an all-embracing, all-encompassing, and fundamental call to relationship whereby each person finds his or her own identity and relates to other human beings. The fundamental dynamism between the sexes enables individuals to specify themselves in their own proper sexual roles. This ability to relate interpersonally is a constitutive element of personality. Human sexuality is not determined by biology, but by a relational life carried on within the concrete experience of a particular culture. Human sexuality is a task to be accomplished in the interpersonal give and take of the multiple relationships that people enjoy.[37] Any study of human sexuality must investigate all levels and not stop at the biological substratum, as does *Humanae Vitae.*

For Christian couples, sexual love ought to emerge essentially as charity (*agape*),[38] a charity that is expressed physically. Love in the order of intention is directed from person to person, but love as an intentional relationship seeks some sort of corporeal sign: a look, a gesture, a touch. A human person is a being who must incarnate his or her love in and by the flesh. Married persons express their gifts of self to one another by means of sexual intercourse.

Not only does conjugal love unite husband and wife, it likewise expresses this union by means of procreation. A child ought to be the fruit of love expressed in the context of the conjugal act. While we note this relation between procreation and mutuality, this is not to say that every concrete expression of conjugal love must be open to procreation. This is *not* the ultimate question. I maintain, rather that the marriage as a whole must be open to life: This is the heart of the matter.

When we consider a marriage as a lifetime process, an ongoing task, we cannot isolate individual actions, ascribing moral goodness or badness to each of them. Rather, emphasis should be placed on the moral patterns that develop within a marriage: Is the couple developing a contraceptive attitude, a selfish attitude, a hedonistic attitude?[39]

Fertility, in and of itself, is premoral. It takes on either a moral or immoral dimension when considered within the context of a marital situation.[40] Thus we consider fertility in one light when it is experienced by a young couple with ample resources, and in another light when it is experienced by a couple with many children and a history of painful birth experiences ranging from psychic duress to physical fatality.

And so, with many Catholic theologians, I am convinced that it is morally lawful for an individual couple, who love children and wish to be as generous as possible in accepting children as the fruit of their love for each other, to express their love by intercourse even when, at times (limited or extended), they must, because of certain conditions (such as psychological or physical health, finances, number of children, etc.) take care to avoid a new pregnancy by means determined by conscience.

QUESTIONS FOR DISCUSSION

1. Why would some people consider contraception as an intrinsic evil?

2. Do you think that we can equate the will of God and my biological structure? Give some concrete examples.

3. What does it mean "to transmit life"?

4. Do you feel that people today are responsible enough to make their own decisions for or against parenthood?

7

Contraceptive Methods— A Medico-Moral Look

After exploring the thought of the church as expressed in *Humanae Vitae,* we now turn our study to the situation of those couples who have decided that they need to regulate births. What methods are available? How does a couple reach the desired end? In light of the inverse relationship between effectiveness and safety, what limitations are placed upon couples seeking to space or limit births?

Contraception can be achieved by preventing any of the conditions necessary for pregnancy to occur.[1] We will now examine some of these forms of prevention.

I. NATURAL PLANNING METHODS

These methods of avoiding pregnancy are based upon an effort to understand and observe the rhythms of nature and do not involve the use of any artificial means of contraception.

A. The Rhythm Method

With this method, a couple refrains from intercourse during that part of the woman's menstrual cycle when a fertilizable egg is available.

The menstrual cycle lasts, in principle but not often in fact, for 28 days. Variations from 18 to 40 days are possible. During this cycle, the egg is available for fertilization for approximately one day, namely the 24 hours that follow ovulation. Since there is no direct sign of ovulation, however, the time of its occurrence must be estimated.[2] Ovulation typically occurs halfway between the menstruations, on about the 15th day, but a woman's menstrual cycle is seldom perfectly regular. In most women, menstruation is erratic following the birth of a baby, and at least 25% of all women always experience fairly erratic cycles.[3] Moreover, some women after a long record of regular menstruation, may suddenly become irregular.

Even when menstruation is regular, ovulation can occur anywhere from 16 to 12 days before the start of the next menstruation, and is sometimes induced by the stimulus of sexual intercourse. Finally, sperm can live in the woman's cervix for up to 72 hours and sometimes longer, so that even if intercourse occurs four days before ovulation it may, on rare occasions, cause conception.

1. Regular Menstruation   When a woman menstruates regularly every 28 days, ovulation will most likely occur on the 15th day of the cycle, but can happen anytime from the 13th to the 17th days—a period of five days. Since, we have said, sperm can live for 72 hours or even longer, the four days prior to ovulation are also unsafe. This gives a couple a total of ten days each month that are unsafe for intercourse, namely from the 9th to the 18th days inclusive. Although some women have cycles as short as 21 days or as long as 38 days, this matters little so long as it is a regular pattern. If conception is to be prevented, the couple must abstain from intercourse for a period of ten days, starting 20 days before the next menstruation is expected.

2. Irregular Menstruation   A woman with irregular menstrual periods must keep an accurate record of her menstrual cycle for a year and then note the shortest and longest cycles. This woman would then subtract 19 from the number of days in her shortest cycle and ten from the number of days in her longest cycle.

As we have stated, the rhythm method is based on the principle that the egg, once it has been shed from the ovary, is only capable of fertilization for a short time, and once this time has passed, there is no possibility of conception until the next ovulation. While the principle is sound, the practice is difficult and susceptible to error. The technique involved depends upon a rough prediction of a future, and therefore uncertain, event.

B. The Basal Body Temperature Method

After ovulation the temperature of a woman's body rises slightly, perhaps one-half of one degree, due to the rise in the metabolic rate. Once this temperature rise is detected, it should

71

then be safe for intercourse to occur.[4] To discern the temperature accurately, it must be taken immediately upon waking. Prior to taking her temperature the woman must be at rest for at least one hour and she cannot smoke or drink. The temperature must be taken before any activity, including getting out of bed. A rectal thermometer is preferable, because it is more accurate.

This method is retrospective, that is, it records and interprets. But the readings that are charted are easy to misread, the changes are slight, and the readings can easily be confused by illness or stress. For example, a slight head cold, flu, anxiety, or stress could alter the reading.

C. Periodic Abstinence

Some maintain that the sexual discipline of periodic abstinence imposed by the rhythm method gives security to the marriage by demonstrating that each partner is capable of control over his or her sexual drive. Abstinence, the proponents maintain, promotes the development of sexual maturity, providing an opportunity for conjugal love to be demonstrated in ways other than intercourse. This demonstration of concern for the spouse and for the family which overrides desire for physical gratification, produces psychological benefits that flow to other members of the family.[5]

While it is true that the self-discipline required for correct use of the rhythm method might not impair a healthy marriage, it can wreck a poor marriage by surfacing some latent problem. I see yet another and deeper level for concern, however. Periodic abstinence seemingly destroys the spontaneity of the sexual act. The spouses are ruled by the menstrual cycle. Physical pleasure is reduced to a force that must be controlled or harnessed.

As we have already stated, biological law is not synonymous with divine law. Ideally the sexual act ought to be performed within an atmosphere of freedom and spontaneity. It should not be restricted to certain times of the month because of a biological rhythm only. The temporal barrier can be as morally repugnant as the spatial or chemical barrier.[6] If we affirm that human sexuality is personal, and not just appetite, however, then the sacrifice involved here need not always be seen as a cruel or inhuman deprivation.

It must also be mentioned that two medical complications are sometimes associated with the prolonged practice of periodic abstinence. In the first place, ectopic pregnancies may follow conception that takes place late in the cycle. The failure to inhibit the next period can lead to the consequent displacement of the ovum to an extra-uterine site or the abnormal intrauterine attachment know as *placenta previa*.[7] Secondly, the systematic disjunction of the time of ovulation and the time of coitus means that accidental conception will most likely involve either an aging ovum or a deteriorating sperm, which significantly increases the chances of embryonic abnormalities such as anencephaly and spina bifida.[8]

D. The Ovulation Method

According to Dr. Billings, who originated the ovulation method, conception depends not only upon ovulation, but upon the presence of a particular type of mucus that a woman can recognize. Thus, with this method, the regulation and control of ovulation are completely unnecessary.[9]

After instruction in the interpretation of the pattern of mucus secretion that accompanies a fertile ovulation a woman can determine her days of infertility and possible fertility.[10] The system is applicable in all circumstances throughout the reproductive life, since it does not require that the menstrual cycle be regular nor does it depend upon medication.

In a menstrual cycle of average length there is no apparent secretion of vaginal mucus for a number of days after the period has ended. These are known as the dry days, and these are safe for intercourse. As the cycle progresses, an amount of mucus secretion can be detected. The mucus changes appearance and produces a different sensation as ovulation approaches.[11]

When it first appears the mucus is cloudy, white or yellow, and has a sticky sensation. Close to ovulation the mucus becomes clear and slippery and stretches without breaking, similar to the white of a raw egg. Ovulation occurs soon after the clear, slippery peak symptom.[12] The period should then follow in about two weeks. Thus this method can be used to avoid pregnancy or determine fertility.

The peak symptom is accompanied by vulval fullness and swelling which, together with the sensation of lubrication, contribute to increased sexual inclination. Hormonal influences are also important in this regard.

The advantage of this method of determining fertility is that the woman is not forced to rely upon her memory; she is reminded by the symptoms. If a woman does become pregnant, she can even pinpoint the act of intercourse that caused it.

While there are no pathological difficulties with this method, it too exerts the pressure of periodic abstinence. Intercourse, ideally, should be the climax of mutual love expressed freely without the limitations of a time frame. But the mature couple must ask themselves which undesirable situation they prefer: temporary abstinence or an unwanted pregnancy. If a couple can live with abstinence during the time of ovulation, when the sexual urge in the female is at its height, all well and good; otherwise this method may cause undo stress and frustration. Another point to be considered is that the method of observation leaves room for error. Even with education in this regard, interpretation of symptoms can be a risky business.[13]

Temporal barriers imposed on the basis of temperature, menstrual indications, or cervical mucus serve to establish a rather artificial context for the enjoyment of sexual relations. Moreover, the effectiveness of the rhythm method is low, and I maintain that, while the ovulation method shows promise, it needs more study.[14]

E. Coitus Interruptus

Coitus interruptus means the withdrawal of the penis before the male orgasm so that ejaculation occurs outside the vagina. While this is, perhaps, one of the earliest forms of birth control, less than 5% of all couples in the United States today use this as the only method of contraception. It is a rather unreliable method, mainly because it is extremely difficult to judge the exact moment ejaculation begins, and the small quantity of seminal fluid that sometimes precedes the main volume of the ejaculate very often contains sperm. It is also argued that the sudden interruption of intercourse immediately prior to its climax may be psychologically harmful if practiced over a long period of time.[15]

This method does have the advantage of costing nothing, and of requiring no medical attention or supervision. It may, however, cause undo psychological tension for both male and female,[16] and, as with other natural methods, *coitus interruptus* can destroy the spontaneity of the lovemaking experience.

II. MECHANICAL METHODS

The two most common mechanical methods of contraception are the condom and the diaphragm.

A. Condom

The condom is said to have been invented by Gabrielli Fallopio in the 16th century with the intention of preventing the spread of venereal diseases rather than controlling pregnancy.[17]

When properly used, the condom gives a high degree of contraceptive protection, and is even more effective when used with a chemical. Probably the greatest source of failure with the condom occurs when a man allows his erection to subside while the penis is still inside the vagina. In this situation a certain amount of semen can easily leak around the rubber ring at the end of the condom and seep into the vagina.

Some couples find the use of a condom to be an embarrassment, since it can only be put on when the man has an erection, often calling for the interruption of love play. Of course, with a bit of imagination, it is possible to incorporate the application of the condom into the act of love making. Another drawback is that either partner may find that the condom dulls sensation or feels unpleasant. A recent innovation in the condom market has sought to offset this problem by replacing the rubber condom with a lambskin, lubricated condom.

The major virtue of the condom is that it is easily obtainable from nonclinical sources and can be used without medical supervision. In a limited range of cases the use of the condom is clinically advised. These include cases of vaginal trichomoniasis and moniliasis where there is the likelihood of re-infestation, or cases of premature ejaculation in which the use of the condom may be effective in prolonging coitus.

It would seem that the condom is the most practical method of contraception for couples whose acts of intercourse are sporadic or unpredictable.

B. Diaphragm

The diaphragm is like the steam locomotive: It was first in the field, it brought emancipation to millions, and for a long time it had no rivals. It still has some supporters, but its use has seesawed over the years.

The diaphragm is a dome-like rubber device with a coiled spring contained within the rim. The device fits across a woman's cervix to act as a physical barrier to sperm. By itself, the cap is not particularly safe but, when used in conjunction with spermicides, it can be quite effective.[18]

The insertion of a diaphragm is not very difficult, but it does require practice and instruction. The woman holds the edges of the device together, and pushes it by hand into the vagina so that the bottom edge rests against the rear of the vagina and the top edge rests against the vaginal wall behind the bladder. The spring causes the diaphragm to retain its circular shape, holding it in place. Before insertion, some spermicidal cream or jelly is squeezed on the inside of the cap. The cap can be placed in the vagina not more than two to three hours before intercourse. After intercourse it needs to be left in place for at least six to eight hours while the sperm die. If intercourse occurs again during that time, more spermicide has first to be introduced into the vagina without disturbing the cap.

Diaphragms vary in size. An initial fitting by a doctor is essential, and the cap has to be checked for fit every six months, after a pregnancy, or if more than ten pounds have been gained or lost. At home, the cap must be washed thoroughly and checked for holes.

Some women may find the insertion of the diaphragm a messy procedure, but this difficulty has been lessened by devices known as diaphragm introducers which can facilitate the correct insertion and withdrawal of the cap.

One of the objections to the diaphragm is that its insertion and use can interfere with the spontaneity of lovemaking. One must plan intercourse so that the cap can be placed in position in advance. In recent years, however, due to conflicting reports about the safety of oral contraceptives, many doctors have returned to prescribing this form of birth control for their patients.

III. CHEMICAL CONTRACEPTIVES

Most contemporary vaginal contraceptives rely on both chemical and physical properties for effectiveness. The spermicidal component, which immobilizes the spermatozoa, is invariably combined with a gelatinous or oleaginous base that forms a barrier to penetration and provides a vehicle to carry the spermicide. Among these chemical contraceptives are suppositories, tablets, jellies, creams, foams, pastes, aerosols, and C-Film (a small square of spermicide-impregnated plastic that can be inserted in the vagina or on the penis before entrance).

Quite a number of spermicides have appeared on the market that are designed to be used alone rather than in conjunction with a diaphragm. These spermicides differ greatly in their odor and consistency, and people must experiment to find the one best suited to their needs. Some people may find that the extra lubrication these chemicals provide is an advantage, while others may find it a nuisance. Generally speaking, the chemicals are much less effective than either the condom or diaphragm,[19] and some people develop irritation from their use.

IV. INTRA-UTERINE DEVICE (IUD)

The IUD is a small plastic device designed for insertion into the uterus where it may remain for several years, allowing intercourse to occur without restriction. While in place, it works as an effective contraceptive, although some doctors recommend the use of a spermicide around the time of ovulation. Once the IUD is removed, fertility returns within a year.[20]

The reason for the effectiveness of the IUD has not been clearly established. Some say the device makes the ovum pass down the Fallopian tube too rapidly for either fertilization or implantation. Others maintain that the IUD interferes with the lining of the uterus, so that implantation cannot take place. Still a third group states that the IUD interferes directly with the implantation process. Since it is not established whether the IUD acts as a contraceptive or an abortifacient special caution should be exercised in making a moral decision regarding its use. A further moral consideration with the IUD arises when one questions whether or not a human being is present prior to implantation. We will explore this problem later in our study.

Lippes Loop and Saf-T Coil are the most commonly used IUDs for women who have had children already. For those who have not, the Copper 7 or Copper T are the most common. Other IUDs include Margulies Spiral, Birnberg Bow, Grafenberg Ring, and Zipper Ring.[21]

The modern IUD comes in several different sizes and shapes. In order to introduce the IUD into the uterus, the doctor stretches it out to a long, thin shape and passes it through the cervical canal. Once it is inside the womb the IUD returns to its original shape. The process of insertion may be slightly uncomfortable, but if the woman is relaxed there is ordinarily little pain. If there are no complications such a device can be left in place for several years.

One risk with the IUD, even with proper medical insertion, is that some women tend to expel the device from the uterus through the vagina, sometimes without realizing what has happened. This is more apt to occur during the first few months of use or at the time of menstruation. It is recommended that women who have not had children avoid use of the IUD since the risk of expulsion and the pain and bleeding known as menorrhagia are more common among them.[22] After the first IUD is inserted a woman will probably experience some discomfort, usually in the form of greater period pains and longer, heavier periods. After a few months these symptoms generally subside, although loss of blood during the period may be heavier than before. After the first preliminary exams the doctor should check the IUD annually. Also, the devices have a thread attached which hangs an inch or so into the vagina to allow the woman to check herself and the position of the IUD.

Another side-effect of the IUD is that it may provoke a minor irritation that can lead to infection of the womb if not treated. In such a situation, the woman may experience pain, backache, and probably a discharge of mucus. Obviously, medical attention should be sought. Another lesser risk is perforation of the uterus.

How reliable is the IUD? When used by women who have ready access to medical care, the IUD is second in effectiveness only to the oral pills.

Some pregnancies, however, have occurred even with the IUD in place. In such rare cases the IUD will not interfere with the baby's development or birth, although it is better to remove the device in order to lessen the risk of miscarriage.

V. Minor Methods of Contraception

Other methods of contraception, some rather bizarre, have been employed over the years. These include vaginal douching, which basically involves the flushing of the vaginal tract immediately after intercourse; *amplexus reservatus,* in which no ejaculation takes place at all; *coitus saxonicus,* a method in which the man exerts pressure on his perineum when he is at the point of ejaculation so that the spermatozoa is refluxed into the bladder; the use of a gamic male appliance, which consists of a small rubber bag attached to the end of a thin rubber tube that is pushed down the urethra of a man's penis so that when he ejaculates the semen is held in the bag; and a technique known as "holding back" in which the woman refrains from orgasm (a practice based on the mistaken notion that a female seed is released at the moment of climax).

VI. ORAL CONTRACEPTIVES

No other form of contraception has been so revolutionary as the pill. It is easy to use, reversible, and 99% effective. The pill uses synthetic forms of the hormones estrogen and progesterone,[23] which are produced normally in the body for a few days in each menstrual cycle and continuously during pregnancy. These hormones inhibit the output of FSH and LH hormones which are needed if follicles are to ripen for ovulation. The contraceptive pill, therefore, prevents ovulation so that no ovum is available for fertilization by sperm.

The term "the pill" is actually a misnomer since there are basically three types of pills: *combination,* in which each active pill in the package contains both hormones; *sequential,* in which three-quarters of the active pills contain just enough estrogen and only the rest contain both hormones; and *continuous,* in which all pills contain only progesterone. We also might mention here the so-called "morning-after pill." This pill, which contains a large dose of estrogen, is taken about three days after unprotected intercourse. The estrogen affects the uterine lining and implantation is prevented. The pill thus serves as an abortifacient with harmful side effects.

A. Combination Pill

This group of pills, which is the most widely used today, includes Anovlar, Conovid, Lyndiol 2.5, Ortho-Novin, Ovulen, Norelstrin, Previson, and Volidan. The woman takes one standard pill each day for 21 days, starting on the fifth day after menstruation begins and ending on the 25th day. There is a gap of seven days during which no hormone is taken and menstruation occurs; then a new package is started.

The combination pill, in addition to preventing ovulation, affects the uterine lining so that implantation cannot occur, and causes the cervical mucus to thicken, forming a chemical barrier to the sperm.

B. Sequential Pill

This group of pills includes Feminor, Sequens, and Serial 28. This type of pill is closer to a woman's cycle, but is less effective. The woman takes 21 pills, starting on the fifth day after menstruation. The first 14 pills contain estrogen only; the rest contain both hormones. Ovulation is prevented, but there is no effect on the uterine lining or cervical mucus.

C. Continuous Pill

There are 28 pills of this type for each cycle, and one is taken every day, even during menstruation. All are active and contain only synthetic progesterone. This pill works mainly by affecting the uterine wall lining and cervical mucus, rather than by preventing ovulation.

D. Depo-Provera

This method of birth prevention is based on hormonal principles similar to those for the oral pill. In this case, however, 150 mg. of the hormones are injected every three months or larger doses are given every six months. This method has been used, for the most part, in underdeveloped and overpopulated areas. It is very effective, but causes several side effects including the disruption of menstrual bleeding, vomiting, dizziness, moodiness, headache, weight gain, and rectal bleeding.

E. The Side Effects

Most women experience a few side effects from the pills. While some of these are merely unpleasant, others can be dangerous. Some side effects, similar to symptoms that women experience during pregnancy, may be only temporary: tenderness in the breasts, nausea and vomiting, weight gain or loss, bloating, leg cramps, etc. A spotty darkening of the skin, especially on the face, is possible and may persist. There may be unexpected vaginal bleeding or changes in the menstrual period which should be reported to the doctor.[24]

The physician may find that the levels of sugar and fatty substances in the woman's blood are elevated by the pills. The long term effects of these changes are still under study. There are other reactions which have not yet been proven to have a cause-effect relationship with the pill: dizziness, nervousness, some loss of scalp hair, increase in body hair, increase or decrease in sex drive, change in appetite.

Obviously, no woman should take any form of contraceptive pill without the advice of her physician. All pills, especially the high estrogen ones, carry a risk of blood clotting that may threaten life. Clots occasionally form in the blood vessels of the legs and pelvis of apparently healthy people. These may threaten life if the clots break loose and then lodge in the lung or if they form in other vital organs, such as the brain. It has been estimated that each year one woman in 2,000 on the pill suffers a blood clotting disorder severe enough to require hospitalization. The estimated death rate from abnormal blood clotting in healthy women under 35 who are not taking the pill is one in 500,000; whereas for the same number taking the pill the rate is one in 66,000.[25] For healthy women over 35 not taking the pill, the rate is one in 200,000 compared to one in 25,000 for pill users. Blood clots are about three times more likely to occur in women over the age of 34.[26]

For these reasons it is important that women who have had blood clots in the lung, legs, or brain not use oral contraceptives. Anyone using the pill who has severe leg or chest cramps, coughs up blood, has difficulty in breathing, experiences sudden severe headache or vomiting, dizziness or fainting, disturbance in vision or speech, weakness or numbness of an arm or leg, should discontinue the pill immediately and see a physician.

Before the pill is prescribed other disorders, such as hepatitis, diabetes, migraine, and epilepsy, must be made known to the physician. At this stage there is no proof that the pill can cause cancer, but estrogen can aggravate some forms of existing cancer. Cervical smears are an important part of the medical examination that accompanies the pill, and a cancerous condition can thus be found in time.

Doctors still disagree as to how long a woman should stay on the pill. On the average, women tend to use it for three to four years. Although a woman regains fertility by ceasing to take the pill, it may be some time before her ovaries are functioning normally and conception can occur.

VII. CONTROLS ON MALE FERTILITY

A suitable male contraceptive is difficult to achieve because while it should suppress the male's fertility it must not diminish his libido or potency. Also, it must not have any obviously feminizing effects, and it should be reversible.

Some promising approaches to this need range from antifertility vaccines that could immunize a man against his own sperm to the direct application of ultrasound to the testicles. Before an anti-sperm vaccine becomes a reality, solutions must be found to possible genetic damage, injury to germ cell tissue, and antiimmunization reaction.[27]

Some real excitement has been generated by the experiments of Dr. Mostafa Fahim of the Columbus School of Medicine at the University of Missouri. Dr. Fahim has been researching male contraception by a method that raises testicular temperature by means of ultrasound. It is a method that in time promises to be effective, inexpensive, and painless. It requires no surgery and will take only ten minutes.[28]

VIII. CONCLUDING REFLECTIONS

Regarding methods of contraception, the legitimate diversity of opinion that exists in the present state of the question should be recognized and admitted. Confessors and counselors should not impose any position in an absolutely binding way. Their task is rather to assist people in arriving at a responsible decision.

When a couple has decided on sound moral grounds to limit their family, pastoral concern should help them see in their sexuality a way of realizing those values that build a community of love. If their sexuality serves this purpose by making them more sensitive, thoughtful, understanding, and loving then their decision can be seen as moral. If, on the contrary, contraception leads to greater self-centeredness, preoccupation with pleasure, exploitation, break-down of moral character, and infidelity or hedonism, then it is not wholesome and is immoral.

In short, we have to ask what values are being affirmed and what values are being denied by the use of contraceptives. These considerations ought to be weighed by the couple in consultation with a priest and a physician so that the best possible decision can be reached and so that the safest method may be proposed for their use.

QUESTIONS FOR DISCUSSION

1. From a philosophical point of view it seems that the so-called natural methods of birth regulation are governed by a temporal barrier while the

so-called artificial methods are governed by a spatial barrier. Do you see a distinction here? If so, what?

2. Given the possibility that chemical contraceptives might be harmful to one's health, should one ever use such a method? Would this situation be similar to that of smoking cigarettes?

3. Discuss acceptable means of achieving birth regulation in overpopulated countries.

4. Discuss the role that abstinence can play within a love relationship. Is it always a form of deprivation?

8

Responsible Parenthood

As was noted earlier, the encyclical *Humanae Vitae* was not so much a study of the issue of birth control in and of itself, as an authoritative affirmation of the position of the church on marriage and procreation, a position that had undergone numerous developments over the years.

Vatican II set the direction for future preservation of the unitive and procreative meanings of marriage.[1] The genuine relationship between these meanings is harmed or even destroyed whenever the conjugal act sinks to the level of sexual exploitation. It makes little difference whether this exploitation occurs in an effort to conform with biological laws and rhythms or to disregard them. An irresponsible act of procreation can destroy the bond that is central to a marriage just as easily as can the irresponsible use of a contraceptive technique.[2]

I. RESPONSIBILITY

A couple who strives to grow in mutual affection and to promote unity and stability in their lives, is not only strengthening the bond of love between them, but readying themselves for the vocation of parenthood. When a husband and wife consciously ready themselves to bring children into the world and educate them, I would say they are preserving the unitive and mutual components of marriage.

When a couple observes total continence due only to an absolute reverence for improperly functioning, changing, or unknown biological laws and rhythms, a marriage can be undermined. Nor is the procreative good obtained by an act of procreation that is contrary to genuine human responsibility. The couple, drawing upon their shared experience, must decide whether or not total continence carries greater risks for conjugal fidelity and generous fecundity than would a moderate use of some artificial means of birth regulation.[3]

II. GROUNDS FOR DECISION-MAKING

Vatican II required of spouses the realization that through the powers of procreation they are called to a joint venture as "cooperators with the love of God" and "interpreters of that love."[4] This call implies a generous openness and willingness to accept the task of parenthood. At the same time it imposes on parents a sober realization that they must assume personal responsibility for determining the manner and extent of the procreative response.

Thus an attitude that says "Let's leave it all in the hands of God and accept whatever he sends" is both simplistic and morally irresponsible. Responsible parenthood demands recognition of those situations and conditions where it would be irresponsible and, hence, immoral to beget children. A couple is called to the task of procreativity not propagation.[5] In other words, the creative plan of God in which they are called to share is rational and not capricious. The interpretation of that plan lies in the sphere of personal conscience and not biological integrity.

Responsible parenthood requires that spouses not insist that the church, or a priest, or a doctor make their decisions for them. The thinking of Vatican II is quite clear: "The parents themselves, and no one else, should ultimately make this judgment in the sight of God."[6]

In view of the broad meaning of sexuality that I have established in this book, it is obvious that the decision to have or not to have a child must be based on a wide spectrum of considerations. The physical, emotional, and psychological wellbeing of the wife, the husband, and the already existing family must be an important factor in this decision. The welfare of members of the family with special needs, for example retarded or handicapped children, cannot be overlooked either. Vatican II openly suggested that parents take a long-range view of their responsibilities, being sensitive to the added demands that new children may bring.[7]

Together with the economic situation of the individual family, the conditions of society must also be considered. Concern for underpopulation as well as overpopulation must be faced honestly and realistically. In short, the call to responsible parenthood means that the decision regarding family size must reflect concern not only for the desires and needs of the individual parents and family, but for the well-being of society as a whole.

Responsible reasons for limiting one's family are many and complex. One or another consideration may not be sufficiently strong in and of itself, but taken together with other factors it may provide the basis for a responsible moral conviction that a family should be limited.[8] Although husband and wife together must ultimately accept the responsibility for such a judgment, the complexity of such a decision warrants the advice and support of a prudent and sensitive priest or counselor. The appropriate role of a priest is to assist a couple in making a prudent, responsible decision and to support them in its implementation.

III. SUPPORT FOR RESPONSIBLE PARENTHOOD

The following principles support the philosophy just described.

A. Person-centered Morality

As is indicated in the *Pastoral Constitution on the Church, (Gaudium et Spes)*, the moral evaluation concerning family limitation must be made "in light of the total welfare of the persons involved."[9]

B. Biblical Teaching on Moral Matters

Those passages in the bible which, in the past, were cited as prohibiting contraception, have been seriously misinterpreted. We need only remind ourselves of the famous so-called sin of Onan and its connection with *coitus interruptus*. Careful study of the New Testament strongly supports placing the locus of moral judgment on the total person and his or her relationships rather than on an analysis of the physical act of the moment.[10]

C. Renewed Understanding of Natural Law

We have noted a movement away from a static, predominantly biological understanding of natural law to a more dynamic interpretation of it as our rational, historical participation in God's plan. From this perspective, the basis for moral judgment does not lie in actions that are intrinsically predetermined as evil, but in the response of the person to the call of God in the concrete realities of daily life.[11]

D. Scientific and Medical Advances

Significant advances in research and technology have increased our ability to understand and our responsibility to become cooperators with and interpreters of the love of God in the task of transmitting life.[12]

These advances serve as a challenge to our freedom and responsibility. Obviously, not all that is new is good. We must exercise the gift of prudence in deciding whether or not to use new methods and means of cooperation.

E. Influence of Behavioral Sciences

The problem that we face today is that of overpopulation. Rapidly changing social and economic conditions in recent decades, a greater sensitivity to the world population explosion, and a growing concern for improved standards of living have brought many entirely new elements to bear on the decision concerning responsible procreation.[13]

Couples today must take into account the fact that our geographical world is shrinking, that our food supply is not unlimited. Yet we cannot assign by law the number of children permitted to each family. The responsibility lies, not with government, but with the responsible couple.

F. Theology of Conjugal Love

Vatican II emphasizes the centrality of conjugal life and love and does not envision procreation as the only reason for sexual relations. Nor does it see sexual relations as a means of satisfying lust. The theology of conjugal love needs to be explored so that we may learn to view marriage in a personalist perspective. Procreation is not merely prolongation of the species, but cooperation with God. Finally, the method of family limitation chosen must respect the total nature of the person.

Responsible family planning, therefore, attempts to control fertility in order to serve the good of the wider community as a whole, the family as a unit, and individual family members in particular. Discernment, judgment, and sincere love are the key guides for parents. Obviously, every decision made from love will involve sacrifice.

Generally speaking, parents must balance with care, effort, and foresight a basic trust in the past, the future, and themselves. Since each family lives a different reality, each family must make its own unique decisions. Numbers, rules, and blueprints are impossible; even ideals can be misleading.[14] Love must serve, but the power to decide when children are to be born and how many of them there will be gives a new dimension to that service of love.

The approach of Vatican II towards responsible parenthood leads to certain conclusions. First, when the physical processes of nature have been so disordered that new pregnancies can be a real physical threat to the mother's life and health she has the right to avoid conception for the sake of her selfpreservation and the greater good of family stability. Second, the statements of Vatican II recognize that many social and psychological disorders are also beyond the control of the individual family and hence can make additional children a threat to the social health of the family. And third, a new recognition of social reality is matched by a new understanding of personal, psychological reality.

I maintain that fertility control must not destroy the sexual unity of the partners. An attitude of intelligent, responsible parenthood must not give way to a manipulative, selfish contraceptive attitude. For that reason I encourage married people to dialogue in the sacrament of reconciliation about their attitude and approach to family planning. While very often it may not be a question of serious sin, it is good for a person to check his or her attitude to see whether or not the conditions that originally led to a decision to practice contraception are still the same. In this light we conclude our thoughts with the sobering words of Pope Paul VI in *Humanae Vitae:*

> It is also to be feared that man, growing used to the employment of anti-conceptive practices, may finally lose respect for woman, and no longer caring for her physical and psychological equilibrium, may come to the point of considering her as a mere instrument of selfish enjoyment, and no longer as his respected and beloved companion.[15]

Questions for Discussion

1. Do you see a contradiction in fact between the thought of Vatican II on responsible parenthood and the position of Pope Paul VI in *Humanae Vitae?*

2. What factors should a couple take into consideration before making a decision regarding the spacing of births?

3. Discuss the distinction between propagation and procreation.

4. What distinction can be made between contraception and fertility regulation?

5. What relationship do you see between the decision to practice contraception and the reception of the Sacrament of Reconciliation?

9

The Issue of Sterilization

Sterilization is the irreversible termination of the capacity for reproduction.[1] As a method of family planning, it was virtually unknown during biblical times. As a result, we would search in vain to find in the bible any explicit references to the morality of such a procedure. The bible does not support any absolute condemnation of sterilization as such.

I. THEOLOGICAL PERSPECTIVE: PRONOUNCEMENTS OF THE MAGISTERIUM

By reviewing some of the theological pronouncements that have been made by the church regarding this issue, we can gain an insight into the moral implications involved.

A. *Casti Connubii* (December 31, 1930)[2]

The encyclical condemned *eugenic* sterilization, i.e. the sterilization of genetically defective persons performed on a large scale. The document asserted as well that private individuals are not free to destroy or mutilate their members except when no other provision can be made for the total good of the person involved.

B. Response of the Holy Office (March 21, 1931)[3]

The Holy Office, when asked what was thought of the so-called eugenic theory, responded that this theory was false. This statement was re-echoed by Pope Pius XI on December 23, 1933 in his *Address to the Sacred College of Cardinals*[4] and again in a further restatement by the Holy Office.[5]

C. Response of the Holy Office (February 24, 1940)[6]

The Holy Office was then asked whether or not direct sterilization could ever be licit. This question included the possibility of temporary sterilization as well as perpetual sterilization. The Holy Office stated that such a procedure in either case would be against the law of nature.

D. Pope Pius XII *Address to the Midwives* (October 29, 1951)

Here the Holy Father states that sterilization is a grave moral transgression whether seen as a means or as an end result. He says, "Direct sterilization, that is, that which aims at making procreation impossible as a means or end, is a grave violation of the moral law. It is illicit."[7]

E. Pope Pius XII *Address to XXVI Congress of Urologists* (October 8, 1953)

On this occasion Pope Pius XII addressed himself to the issue of sterilization as it applies to the principle of totality. His response revealed a narrow understanding of the principle and a strict interpretation of its application: The principle of totality does not justify the removal of healthy fallopian tubes when pregnancy might be dangerous by reason of disease of the heart, lungs, kidneys ...[8]

F. Majority Report of Papal Commission (July 1966)

As we have already shown, the primary focus of this report was the wider understanding of conjugal love within marriage. The members of the majority did separate the issues of contraception and sterilization by stressing that sterilization was not to be seen as a technique of responsible family limitation. As the report says, "Sterilization is generally to be avoided as a means of responsibly avoiding conception."[9]

G. *Humanae Vitae* (July 18, 1968)

Pope Paul VI restates with vigor the condemnation of sterilization: *Equally to be excluded, as the teaching authority of the Church has frequently declared, is direct sterilization, whether perpetual or temporary, whether of the man or the woman.*[10]

H. *The Ethical and Religious Directives for Catholic Health-Care Facilities* of the N.C.C.B.

This list of directives appeared in November 1972 and addressed the issue of sterilization surgery in Catholic hospitals. The point to note is that this is the first document that offers a wide interpretation of the principle of totality and does not see sterilization in a limited way:

> Procedures that induce sterility, whether permanent or temporary, are permitted when: (a) they are immediately directed to the cure, diminution or prevention of a serious pathological condition and are not directly contraceptive in intent; and (b) a simpler treatment is not readily available.[11]

I. Response of the Holy Office (March 13, 1975)

The Holy Office hoped to curtail a growing interpretation of totality that admitted direct sterilization. In this document the Holy Office spoke against the 1972 *Ethical Directives* to the N.C.C.B.: There is to be no extension of this 1972 principle so as to permit direct sterilization for the total good of the patient.[12]

The Holy Office addressed itself primarily to the question of personal morality and noted that situations may arise where such sterilizing procedures may need to be tolerated on the principle of material cooperation so as to avoid a greater evil.

It must be noted that a clear and decisive majority of theologians writing on the subject today find it difficult to support the restrictive conditions of official teaching in this matter. The issue is hardly closed.

II. AN ANALYSIS OF STERILIZATION

Sterilization can be done for a number of more or less serious reasons, each with its own moral implications. Among the weightier reasons for sterilization are the following.

A. Indirect Sterilization

Medical pathology in the reproductive system that threatens a person's life or health, even apart from further intercourse or pregnancy, could warrant indirect sterilization. An example of this would be the removal of fibroid tumors in the uterus or the removal of the uterus because of cancer. In such cases sterilization could be considered licit based on the principle of proportionate reason. In other words, it is the person's good health that is directly intended in such circumstances with sterilization being an indirect result.[13]

B. Direct Sterilization for Medical Reasons

We are speaking here about a medical pathology in other than the reproductive system that could be aggravated by further pregnancies. Such pathologies would include diabetes and heart disease. The traditional position of the church in such cases is that sterilization is never morally licit because it would be directly intended as a means to secure the good health of the woman.[14]

It must be noted in terms of the classic principle of double effect that the decisive factor is the proportionality between the good and bad effects of the act. At times this proportionality can justify a situation in which the bad aspect of the act procures or produces the good aspect. The good and bad aspects can be so intertwined in the psychology of the person who is intending the act that the physical relationship between the good and bad cannot serve as an adequate norm for the determination of the morality involved.[15]

Any decision applying the principle of totality must be made in a broad context.[16] The reproductive system is not a value to be judged independently of all other values. Thus, direct sterilization could be defended in some cases based on the principle of proportionate reason.

This statement, however, introduces some interesting questions. If sterilization is licit in such cases as those mentioned above, does it make any difference which of the two marriage partners has the sterilizing surgery? I would say here that usually the surgery would be performed on the partner who has the pathological problem.

What should a couple do who feel or know that they might bring genetically defective children into the world? I would recommend that such a couple employ temporary contraceptive methods in the hope that medical science will soon discover a way of dealing with the defect. One could also argue here for permanent sterilization when the likelihood of seriously defective children is very high. In such a situation some say it would be logical to sterilize the partner who carries the defect.

C. Direct Sterilization for Non-medical Reasons

We refer here to direct sterilization as a means of birth control motivated by economic or psychological reasons. Some authors would maintain that these non-medical factors can be weighty enough to warrant direct sterilization, based on the principle of proportionality.

III. STERILIZING TECHNIQUES

From a medical point of view sterilization is the most effective means of contraception that we know of today. There are, however, a variety of procedures involved.

A. Vasectomy

This procedure involves making an incision on both sides of the scrotum above the testicles: an inch of the vas deferens is excised, and the two ends are tied. Since no more sperm can be carried to the seminal vesicles, fertility comes to an end. It must be noted however, that, since there are still sperm present in the seminal vesicles after the operation, it ordinarily takes about six weeks before a man can be sure that he is sterile.

The surgical technique is simple and safe, insofar as any surgery can be considered safe. A vasectomy does not cause impotency nor does it decrease a man's libido. At this point in time we still refer to this surgery as irreversible although efforts are being made to restore fertility through surgical recanalization of the tubes.[17]

B. Orchidectomy

This method, commonly called "castration," involves the removal of the testicles. It often results in a change in secondary sex characteristics which, however, can be controlled by hormone therapy. If performed on an adult the surgery does not necessarily result in impotency.

C. Oophorectomy

This is the surgical removal of both ovaries. After the surgery more ova are produced, so hormone therapy is sometimes needed to prevent changes in the secondary sex characteristics.

D. Salpingectomy

This is the technique by which the fallopian tubes are cut, tied, and resectioned. This technique, often referred to as "tubal ligation" or the "tying of the tubes," is almost 100% effective.

E. Endoscopic Surgery

This involves the use of a laparascope, a fine tube that conducts light and is connected to a telescope. This instrument is inserted through a small cut in the abdomen or vagina and is used to light up and inspect the fallopian tubes. Very fine forceps are inserted and an electrocurrent is passed along them to cauterize the tubes.

F. Hysterectomy

Generally speaking, by this term we mean the surgical removal of the uterus. On a more specific note several types of surgery can be performed: A subtotal hysterectomy involves the removal of the uterus except for the cervix; a total hysterectomy involves the removal of the uterus and cervix; and a radical hysterectomy involves the removal of the uterus, the surrounding tissue, and part of the vagina.

IV. THEOLOGICAL REFLECTIONS

The traditional objection to sterilization is the same as the objection to contraception in general. In other words, this action interferes with the procreative purpose of sexual intercourse. The fundamental evil of sterilization is not the fact that it is mutilation, but that it is considered traditionally as contraceptive mutilation.[18] Thus, even if it is for the total good or health of the individual, sterilization is still considered intrinsically evil and, therefore, may never be employed.

A. Comment on *Humanae Vitae*

This principle is stated in *Humanae Vitae* where Pope Paul VI states that sterilization "may not be willed, intended, or directly performed for any reason."[19] The traditional argument thus maintains that a good end can never justify an evil means and so only indirect sterilization can be allowed.

Contemporary moral theology has found this style of reasoning to be too narrow. Sterilization that represents a rejection, in principle, of the relationship between human sexuality and parenthood, would be considered immoral by most moral theologians today. This would also be the case of contraception that had a similar orientation. But sterilization that is performed to protect some important value would be analyzed under the principle of proportionate reason.[20] Some of these values might include one's health, one's marriage, or even the quality of life to be born.

Practically speaking, we note the difference between sterilization and contraception in the fact that sterilization is relatively permanent. Also, I might point out, that because of its permanence, a vasectomy or tubal ligation undergone before a marriage for the purpose of excluding children would be an attack on the "good of children," and thus would affect the canonical validity of that marriage.[21]

We must distinguish between voluntary sterilization and involuntary sterilization.[22] Take, for example, the case of a retarded girl who has little if any understanding of sexual responsibility: Should she be sterilized for her own good? I would say that no one should ever be sterilized involuntarily for the good of society. I would thus oppose sterilization as a form of punishment for a sex-related crime. But there are cases where it might be in the best interests of the person to submit to sterilization, such as in the case of the retarded girl.

B. A Note on the Magisterial Directive

I would like to take a deeper look at the statement of the Sacred Congregation for the Doctrine of the Faith issued to the N.C.C.B. on March 13, 1975.[23] According to the statement, direct sterilization is always absolutely forbidden because it is intrinsically evil. Furthermore, the principle of totality may not be invoked because sterility intended as such is not directed to the integral good of the person but rather is an assault on his or her ethical good. This is so because sterilization deliberately deprives "foreseen and freely chosen sexual activity of an essential element."[24]

According to Richard McCormick, S.J., the argument of the Congregation as outlined above, rests on a "begging of the question."[25] The Congregational statement is a re-assertion and not an illumination. According to McCormick, no one would quibble with the assertion that an intervention that harms the moral good of the person cannot be justified by the principle of totality. That is obvious from the very meaning of the principle. But what is not clear is that the power to procreate is an element so essential to sexual intimacy that to deprive freely-chosen intimacy of this power is in every instance to assault the ethical or moral good of the person. That is the essential point that is not proven in the statement.[26]

Thus the moral issue at stake is not the understanding and the extension of the principle of totality. Rather, the issue is the reasonableness or unreasonableness of certain surgical or medical interventions that have as their purpose the overall good of the person. From a methodological point of view I would say that direct sterilization is an evil to be avoided insofar as it is possible, but an evil which, until it has been properly placed in the context of its circumstances, remains premoral in character.[27]

Thus the issue is not sterilization as an evil vs. sterilization as a good. Rather, the issue is direct sterilization as intrinsically evil vs. direct sterilization as not intrinsically evil. If we say that sterilization is not intrinsically evil, then some situations of value-conflict will render some cases of sterilization morally permissable.[28]

C. Pastoral Reflections

Sterilization is generally irreversible and thus must be considered as a permanent means of contraception. Morally it differs from other methods of contraception in that it permanently deprives a person of the freedom to respond to the call of parenthood. The moral question is to determine whether one can, with sufficient moral certitude, decide that responsible procreation will never again be a possibility for this person.

As far as decision-making factors are concerned, it is obvious that there are several. The closer a person is to menopause, the more apparent it becomes that one's procreative responsibility is over, hence age is a factor. Also, a serious pathological condition that would make any future pregnancy a serious threat to the life or well-being of the mother could be seen as a proportionately justifying reason, thus medical indications are to be considered. More specifically, a serious risk to the life or well-being of the mother or fetus resulting from obstetrical indications could also be a basis. It must also be noted that clinical evidence can show the possibility of regression or personality damage to a woman in the case of an unwanted or unexpected pregnancy, and so in a limited sense, psychiatric grounds can also be considered. On a lesser scale socio-economic factors can be significant although it must be remembered that a surgical procedure is not the solution to an economic issue.

It seems to me that sterilization is clearly immoral when it represents the irresponsible refusal to fulfill the vocation of husband/wife or father/mother. If a competent physician can determine, in full agreement with his or her patient, that in a particular situation a new pregnancy must be excluded now and forever because it would be thoroughly irresponsible from a medical point of view, then such sterilization might not be opposed to the principles of medical ethics.

QUESTIONS FOR DISCUSSION

1. Discuss the question of sterilization as a certain method of birth control.

2. Discuss the issue of proportionate reason in light of the question of sterilization.

3. Discuss the question of the possibility of marriage for two sterilized individuals.

10

Masturbation

I define masturbation as the stimulation of the genitals by means other than intercourse, usually with the intention of reaching orgasm.[1] Those means are usually the hands, but sometimes other parts of the body may be involved and, especially among females, the use of objects. Masturbation usually involves self-stimulation but not always. According to the classic Kinsey studies (1948-1953), 93% of men and 60% of women who masterbate sought and achieved orgasm.[2] The recent study of Shere Hite indicates a higher percentage of orgasm in female masturbation.[3] Furthermore, according to Kinsey, at least 90% of men and 60% of women masturbate regularly at some time in their lives.[4]

I. AN OVERVIEW OF MASTURBATION

Masturbation has been the subject of more taboos than sexual intercourse. This taboo mentality almost reached the point of social psychosis in the late 19th century when masturbation was associated with everything from acne to laziness, from blindness to insanity. Today these superstitious notions have been debunked. Masturbation is no longer considered to be the cause of any specific physical or mental deterioration. Doctors agree that masturbation as a physical act is harmless. Some sexologists consider masturbation to be a healthy and even a moral practice for teenagers. One eminent sexologist states that "masturbation is like learning how to play a sport—a person must practice."[5]

Moreover, past experiences with masturbation do not seem to cause difficulty when intercourse commences. According to Masters and Johnson, it is not a direct cause of lassitude, premature ejaculation, frigidity, or impotence.[6] In fact, some sexologists believe that masturbation can also play a positive role in successful love-making.

99

These same sexologists add, however, that when adults prefer masturbation to normal intercourse, we are then dealing with an abnormal situation. When this activity becomes the exclusive form of sexual expression, even though there are other alternatives present, it might be termed excessive.

Before contraception became accessible to the majority of people, many looked on masturbation as a necessary alternative to intercourse. In addition, sexologists regard continual masturbation as a normal outlet for adults in certain circumstances: in prisons, in the armed forces, on trips away from home and spouse, during the menstrual period of the wife, and so on. Masturbation has historically been a means of diverting some of the sexual drive. It relieves acute tension that derives from unsatisfactory sex life, or from the temporary absence or inability of a partner. It has also served to ease sexual loneliness in old age.

Masturbation is widely thought to be a physiological transitional stage in the adolescent, and afterwards a byproduct of a healthy sexual impulse, which can act as a safety valve when sexual intercourse is not possible.[7]

II. MASTURBATION: A THEOLOGICAL REFLECTION

Current stands on the morality of masturbation are rooted chiefly in tradition, although certain scriptural texts are commonly cited on the subject.

A. Sacred Scripture

There is no clear, explicit moral prohibition of masturbation in either the Old Testament or the New Testament. However, some classic texts are often cited: Leviticus 15:16, Deuteronomy 23:9-11, Genesis 38, I Thessalonians 4:3-4, Romans 1:24, and I Corinthians 6:10. According to some moralists, the ultimate scriptural word against masturbation is in the following pauline references: I Corinthians 6:9-10, Romans 1:24, Ephesians 5:3-5, and Galatians 5:19-21, but they quickly point out that there is no single technical term in these texts that means "masturbation."[8]

B. Tradition

While the scriptural witness on this issue is nonexistent, the testimony from tradition is quite consistent in viewing masturbation as a serious moral evil, even though the reasons given have varied.

Originally, the deliberate wasting of the seed of life was deemed by most theologians as the principal reason for terming masturbation a grave and intrinsic evil. Thus female masturbation was viewed less severely.[9] Other theologians put greater emphasis on the deliberate pursuit of complete venereal pleasure outside of marriage as the source of evil.[10] Still others considered masturbation as evil because it posed a threat to the propagation of the human race, the presumption being that masturbation reduced the urge to marry and procreate.[11] Most recently, a consensus is emerging that places the malice of masturbation in its being a "substantial inversion of the sexual order of man."[12]

Throughout most of Catholic tradition, every act of masturbation was regarded as gravely and intrinsically evil; if performed with full knowledge and consent, it was considered a mortal sin.[13] During the last decade, however, much discussion has centered around the question of whether or not a single act of masturbation constitutes such a substantial inversion of the sexual order that it must always be regarded as intrinsically grave matter. Most theologians agree that not every deliberately willed act of masturbation necessarily constitutes the grave matter required for mortal sin.[14] I do not mean to imply, however, that masturbation is not potentially sinful or that it can never involve serious sin.

C. Magisterium

We now turn our attention to some of the statements of the church in this matter. Writing in 1054 on various disciplinary situations within the church, Pope Leo IX stated in *De malitia masturbationis* that "masturbators should not be admitted to sacred orders."[15] This position was further strengthened in a decree of the Holy Office in 1679.[16]

It is interesting to note that most of the statements on masturbation come from our own century. We note the 1904 *Decree of the Sacred Penitentiary* which states that the "complete (culminating in orgasm) masturbatory acts of women during the absence of their husbands are gravely illicit."[17] This was followed by a more technical statement made by the Holy Office on August 2, 1929 in which masturbation for the purpose of semen analysis was condemned.[18]

In more recent years we note a constant line of approach. In 1952 Pope Pius XII maintained in *The Christian Education of*

Youth, that adolescent lapses such as masturbation should be seen as grave faults.[19] Ten years later, the Sacred Congregation for Religious stated that "habitual masturbation is an impediment to the religious life."[20] In 1971, the N.C.C.B. *Ethical and Religious Directives* showed its opposition to obtaining seminal specimens through masturbation.[21] The Sacred Congregation for Catholic Education, in its *Guide to Formation in Priestly Celibacy,* stated in 1974 that masturbation is a sign of sexual imbalance.[22] The 1975 statement of the Sacred Congregation for the Doctrine of the Faith, *Persona Humana,* re-affirmed the traditional stance on masturbation.[23] But most recently, the publication of the National Committee for Human Sexuality, *Education in Human Sexuality for Christians,* has moved the discussion forward by incorporating the data of psychology and contemporary moral theology in its approach to masturbation, especially during adolescence.[24]

D. Theological Reflection

There are three basic positions on the morality of masturbation currently in discussion.

1. Masturbation is an objectively grave evil.   According to this, the traditional stance, every act of masturbation constitutes a grave moral de-orientation and is thus a serious sin. However, as *Persona Humana* indicates, mitigating circumstances can help to lesson imputability.[25]

2. Masturbation is objectively neutral.   This position maintains that occasional masturbation is statistically, psychologically, and morally normal.[26] Some educators and psychologists see masturbation as the natural passage from youth to adulthood. Those who hold this view state that masturbation is a perfectly natural outlet and that young people need not fear any pseudo-consequences.

3. Masturbation is symptomatic of many problems.   This position, to which I ascribe, maintains that we must try to discern the moral import of each act of masturbation. Furthermore, it is necessary to distinguish the different forms and levels of masturbation.

a. adolescent masturbation   With the onset of puberty there is curiosity, wonder, fear, and self-discovery, as well as a tendency to close in on oneself. During this period sexuality is not yet oriented toward a partner of the opposite sex, and often the search for release is found in oneself. The adolescent needs self-confidence, support, and direction that will bring reassurance and foster growth and development in reaching out to others. If a parent, confessor, or counselor directs attention to each act of masturbation, it can hamper adolescent growth by increasing the anxiety and feelings of guilt.

b. compensatory masturbation   When youngsters find their healthy growth toward autonomy and personal responsibility repressed or smothered by tyrannical parents or other overprotective people, it is not unusual for them to turn to masturbation.

c. masturbation for necessity   Celibates, married men or women away from home, or spouses who for health or other reasons must abstain from intercourse for long periods of time often find themselves in the predicament of seeking relief from sexual tensions when they are deprived of the normal outlet. The use of masturbation to obtain reasonable relief from excessive tension or to preserve fidelity would seem to be a more prudent choice of values. The moral malice would not be present. However, we might suggest as an alternative the possibility of rechanneling one's sexual energy.

d. pathological masturbation   Psychological maladjustment can at times be the root cause of masturbatory behavior, especially when the impulse becomes a compulsion. This compulsion brings little satisfaction, and yet it is frequently repeated. It is not a syndrome but the symptom of another problem. Involved here is a retardation of psycho-sexual growth. Also, persons who prefer masturbation even in the presence of opportunities for intercourse seem to have a poorly integrated sexuality.

e. medically-indicated masturbation   Masturbation is the standard clinical procedure for obtaining semen for fertility-testing or for diagnosing certain venereal diseases. Such procedures are not a basic abuse of the sexual functions, and hence are not immoral.

f. hedonistic masturbation   Masturbation simply for pleasure alone, without any effort at control or integration can be indicative of self-centeredness, isolation, and evasion of responsibilities to others. Here we are dealing with a fundamental abuse.

III. Pastoral Reflections on Adolescent Masturbation

I maintain that masturbation in and of itself is not an intrinsically evil act. To be properly understood, masturbation must be seen in the context of psycho-sexual development.

During adolescence masturbation is often a way of coping with sexual drives and tensions, a form of experimentation, a symptom of the stage of adolescence itself. Adolescent masturbation may be termed phase-specific sexual activity. It becomes morally wrong when it becomes psychologically harmful.[27]

Masturbation must be seen not as a problem in and of itself but always as an expression or symptom of some interior psychosexual stage. From the onset of adolescence to about 18 years of age, occasional masturbation is statistically, psychologically, and morally normal. This should be seen as developmentally congruent behavior, similar to thumbsucking at an earlier age.[28] It is an attempt on the part of the immature person to cope with new and threatening constellations of drives, pleasures, prohibitions, and pressures.

If the adolescent is to outgrow masturbation, he or she must have an opportunity to develop more mature ways of coping with sexual drives, restrictions, and tensions. In the case of masturbation, as in any other immature reaction, it is far better to appeal to the ego-ideal or ideal self, rather than to the super-ego, in order to motivate behavioral change.[29] Thus masturbation should be treated as any other developmental problem. However, this does not absolve the adolescent from the responsibility of working on the problem. For there is a difference between conscious remorse and anxiety over moral actions,[30] just as there is a difference between the mature acknowledgement that I need to grow, that I need to overcome selfishness, and a feeling of scrupulosity regarding my everyday actions.

The blanket approach toward masturbation in the older teaching of the church was derived from the one-sided physical approach which associated each sexual act with procreation, and an erroneous, almost idolatrous, importance attached to male semen.[31] A more personal approach points out that, ordinarily, masturbation is not that important a matter. There is no blanket gravity that can be assigned to every act of masturbation. Masturbatory activity is generally symptomatic; it often indicates a lack of total integration of sexuality.

QUESTIONS FOR DISCUSSION

1. How should parents and educators approach the subject of masturbation with adolescents?

2. From the point of view of pastoral practice, are most people willing to mention this area of their lives in the context of the sacrament of reconciliation?

3. Discuss the differences in moral evaluation based on the different stages of growth as regards this area.

11

Artificial Insemination

Artificial insemination is the placing of semen in the female's reproductive tract, not by sexual intercourse, but through the use of an instrument, usually a syringe.[1] The purpose of such insemination is to make a marriage fruitful when it is not possible to conceive children through normal intercourse because of some physical condition in the husband or wife.

I. Theological Analysis of AIH

We must make a distinction at the very outset between AIH (*homologous artificial insemination*), which invokes the use of semen from the husband of the woman to be inseminated,[2] and AID (*heterologous artificial insemination*) in which the semen comes from a donor who is not the husband of the woman to be inseminated.[3]

A. Papal Statements

The primary statements on the question of artificial insemination come from Pope Pius XII. On September 29, 1949 he condemned both AIH and AID as immoral in his *Address to the International Congress of Catholic Physicians.*[4] On October 29, 1951, in his *Address to the Congress of the Italian Catholic Union of Midwives,* he restated his position, declaring that artificial insemination depersonalizes the conjugal act, which is highly personal, and is therefore immoral.[5]

In the 1949 statement Pope Pius XII condemned artificial insemination in no uncertain terms. If his condemnation was primarily directed at AID, then we have only to think of the possibility of abuses in sperm banks where sperm is bought and sold. His direct intention was to condemn the anonymous parenthood associated with AID. He did not refer to AIH as destructive of parenthood.

The problem with AIH and AID, as understood by the pope, was that the sperm was obtained by voluntary ejaculation. Prior to the pope's statements, some moralists in the 1940s would have permitted AIH if the semen was obtained in a licit manner:[6] drawing semen from the epididymis in the testicles, or from the vagina after normal intercourse, using a cervical spoon, or using a slightly perforated condom.

Thus there was an increasing permissiveness to AIH from the moralists' viewpoint.[7] The principal moral concern enunciated was that the child should be the fruit of love. This consideration does not seem to be threatened in any way by the biological modification involved in AIH. But other moralists felt that the 1949 statement of Pope Pius XII closed the door on this procedure.[8]

It is therefore necessary to take a closer look at the 1949 statement of Pope Pius XII. According to the pope, AID runs counter to God's plan for marriage, which decrees that husband and wife have exclusive, nontransferable rights to each other's bodies and their generative processes. Within this framework, AID would have to be seen as adultery. Furthermore, the statement indicates that artificial insemination emerges from a false philosophy of life. It assumes that happiness is a "right" and if the couple needs a child for their happiness then the child, too, is their "right."

Obviously both AIH and AID rely on masturbation to procure the semen and masturbation is an intrinsic evil, according to the classical interpretation. Finally, the statement indicates that the social consequences would be disastrous.

B. Jewish and Protestant Opinion

Jewish theological opinion is divided on the issue of AID. Some see it as adulterous; others do not, since there is no genital contact.[9]

Protestant theologians are also divided. On the one hand, we have the contention of Paul Ramsey that the separation of procreation from the husband/wife covenant of fidelity is a violation of the divinely created order of marriage. AID is a breach in the structure of human parenthood, but AIH would be allowed.[10] On the other hand, Joseph Fletcher states that fidelity is a personal bond, and parenthood is a moral relationship, not merely a physical one. Thus for many a childless couple AID may be the most loving act in the situation.[11]

C. The Theological Spectrum

Thus we note the spectrum of attitudes on the issue. The right wing, represented by Pope Pius XII, holds that in God's design human love is procreative. Humans must not put asunder what God has joined together. Just as in contraception, it is wrong to separate procreation from the act of sexual love, so it is equally wrong to separate the act of sexual love from procreation in artificial insemination (either AIH or AID). The left wing, articulated by Joseph Fletcher, stresses that AID can in certain situations be the most loving thing to do. Paul Ramsey seems to hold the middle ground, since he objects to the split between procreation and sexual love in principle, but admits to their separation in individual acts. Thus he sees AIH as moral but AID as immoral.

D. A Theological Evaluation of AIH

Human love is meant to be procreative and responsible, and the child of this union of hearts is meant to be the fruit of this love. Therefore it seems to me that if AIH is not required it would be wrong to use it routinely in place of natural intercourse. But it is not at all clear that the use of AIH in a sterile couple would necessarily turn their marriage into a biological assembly line. This can be seen as the licitness of the exceptional instance.[12]

Today a good number of moralists, such as Bernard Haring, C.Ss.R., Richard McCormick, S.J., and Charles Curran, would not object to a childless couple using AIH even when the semen is obtained by masturbation. Masturbation required for the artificial insemination of one's wife or for semen analysis cannot be morally evaluated solely as a biological event, as we indicated in the previous chapter. It receives its moral significance from the purposes and circumstances of the person involved. Voluntary ejaculation for well-justified diagnostic aims does not constitute ipsation, i.e., a "closing-in" on the self, and self-pleasure.[13]

When the sperm comes from the husband and the marriage is lived in a climate of love, then not only is he biologically the father but there is also the preservation of the unitive and procreative purposes of marriage; there is a moral unity.

I would say that there are no convincing arguments proving either the immorality of the husband's ejaculation in view of fatherhood nor the immorality of introducing the sperm into the wife's uterus. Pastorally speaking, AIH should generally be excluded unless it is the only way an otherwise sterile couple can achieve procreation.[14]

II. AN EXPOSITION OF AID

Standard reasons usually given to justify the use of AID include impotence, sterility, hereditary disease on the part of the husband, or the genital malformation of husband or wife.

A. Legal Issues

Legal problems rarely arise with AIH. Even if Christian opinion is divided about the morality or extension of AIH, still it is not a matter of regulation by civil law.

Problems do arise, however, with AID. For example, we might ask whether AID constitutes adultery under civil law. Adultery is a statutory crime in most American states, though the law is rarely enforced. Most American attorneys would maintain that AID, even without the husband's consent, does not constitute adulterous grounds for divorce.[15]

We then might ask whether a child conceived through AID is legitimate. A model for a law answering this question is the 1966 Oklahoma law which maintains that a child produced through AID is considered naturally conceived and legitimate.[16]

B. Psychological Issues

In the case of AID, the husband undoubtedly has the greater psychological adjustment to make. He could feel that he is deficient, a difficult role in a society that exaggerates the virile image.

Nevertheless, the road for the woman is not always smooth. Somehow she must cope both with her husband's difficulty and with the potential guilt of carrying "another man's baby" in her womb. AID is no magic potion for a shaky, childless marriage.

C. Moral issues

For the purpose of study, it might be wise to ask a series of questions illuminating the moral issues related to AID.

1. Is AID adultery? A strictly legal and physically oriented definition of adultery does not apply to AID, for there is no genital intercourse, no exchange of physical intimacy. But, if AID is not adultery because there is no bodily contact, does it participate in the malicious spirit of adultery by violating the exclusive bond of marriage? Does it violate the bond between procreation and love-making, an essential bond for marriage?

To define sexual fidelity in predominantly physical terms falls far short of an ethos that takes very seriously the contextual meaning of the sexual act of the persons involved. So we must ask: Does AID constitute a gross act of infidelity and a covenant violation?

When AID is freely undertaken with mutual consent, when it is an act of love expressing the inner meaning of the marriage covenant, when it expresses the desire for a child of the wife's own flesh who will be the child of the parenthood covenant of both—it seems that AID would hardly be adultery. It would be infidelity, however, in certain situations, for example, if it were used as an act of revenge against a sterile husband.[17]

2. Is masturbation for the purpose of AIH or AID licit? I have already stated that it would be permissable for AIH. While it is true that the insemination must take place within the context of marital love, the physical act of natural intercourse is not the absolutely necessary expression of that love.

Regarding AID, masturbation would be a medically adequate means, but there is need for donor screening. We have to admit that there are problems here from the point of view of manipulation, since persons will be tempted to use AID for purposes of monetary gain.

3. Is the right to bear children a woman's inherent right? No, not in the absolute sense. Parenthood is not an absolute right.

4. Do psychological factors affect the morality of AID? The theological factors here are central, but they do not exhaust the moral issue. It must be remembered that psychological, social, and legal factors are also vital. The psychological factors do affect the morality. If there are serious and unresolved psychological difficulties about artificial insemination itself or medical problems that would threaten the child, the morality of a decision to proceed must be seriously questioned.

5. Does present legal thinking on AID affect the morality? It must be admitted that, generally speaking, the legal confusion today does add to the difficulty of evaluating the morality of AID. If AID is considered illegal its morality is automatically called into question. If it is declared legal, the doors are opened to its use.

6. Does AID have disastrous consequences? Yes, according to both Pope Pius XII and Pope Paul VI. This response is based on the proposition that AID violates the God-given nature of marriage by divorcing procreation from the act of love, and such a violation of marriage constitutes a threat to the stability and health of society.[18] This response is further based on the proposition that the acceptance of AID amounts to an acceptance of the principle that any technologically feasible separation of procreation from the marriage act can also be acceptable.[19]

Surely human technological pride may become an uncontrollable monster justifying the fears of those who claim that we cannot equate technical progress with human progress. God gives us the awesome freedom to use our technology either to destroy of enhance human life. The problem is that today we live in a grasping, materialistic, consumer-oriented society that is not a healthy atmosphere for the responsible use of freedom. Thus the warnings of Pope Pius XII and Pope Paul VI are to the point.

III. PASTORAL NOTES AND CONCLUSION

In the absence of unresolved and threatening psychological problems, AIH would certainly appear to be a human and Christian moral alternative for a couple. On the other hand, AID raises a whole variety of additional and morally relevant complications.

The presence of socially and legally sanctioned supports for the adoption process makes this route preferable for many couples and, perhaps for many, more responsible. But the lack of adoptable babies and the worries about unknown factors such as the possibility of drug-abuse on the part of many unwed mothers, make adoption highly problematic for many couples. For such people, when their relationship is strong, when their motivations are responsibly sorted out, and when the risks are carefully weighed, AIH *may be* a responsible use of medical technology toward divinely-intended human ends.[20]

As has been mentioned, there is less agreement among moralists with regard to AID. For some theologians such as Fletcher, AID and sperm banks represent the highwater mark of technical achievement. For others such as Ramsey, Haring, and Rahner, AID represents an intrusion into the exclusivity and intimacy of the conjugal bond that unites the couple, making it hard

111

to reconcile AID with the Christian understanding of conjugal love.[21]

It must be mentioned that with AID we also run the risk of possible incest at a later time and genetic abnormality as well. Ramsey views AID as anonymous parenthood that ruptures the marriage bond,[22] while Rahner objects on the grounds that the donor refuses to accept parental responsibility.[23]

Another difficulty with AID lies in the potential threat that the donor-conceived child represents to the husband. The child might well be regarded by such a man as a painful reminder to his impotence or sterility. The child might also be seen as the fruit of an adulterous union, an intrusion into his intimate life.

It can be foreseen that the widespread practice of AID would, in many cases, weaken the relationship between husband and wife. When a woman, after this procedure, becomes conscious of the new life growing within her, she might well realize that she is bearing a child that has no relation to the love that binds her to her partner who, in turn, may feel that he is a stranger to the new child. Thus, with the mainstream of Catholic moralists, I would be very cautious as to the use of AID.

QUESTIONS FOR DISCUSSION

1. Discuss the problematic of masturbation and its relation to AIH-AID. Can you justify the position which allows masturbation for medical reasons?

2. In light of the question of AIH-AID, discuss the right to parenthood? Is it a right? Is it a gift? Is there a limit to the means that can be sought so as to achieve parenthood?

3. Discuss the connection between the unitive and procreative aspects of marriage in light of AID and its separation of spouses.

4. Can you justify the use of AIH in certain situations? Explain.

12

Sex and the Single Catholic

Up to this point in our study we have been treating specific questions that chiefly affect marital morality. We now shift our attention to the single individual. This chapter considers both the experience of the unmarried and the role of sexual relations in the single state.

Although much has been written about the latter, the former area has been little discussed. Scarcely any reference has been made to the single state in the major theological treatises of the leading thinkers in the history of the church. It is not surprising that neither sacred scripture nor the tradition of the church has much to say about the single state when we recall the agrarian culture from which they arose. Yet, in American society today there are more than 41 million single adults.

I. RATIONALE FOR THE SINGLE STATE

Persons freely choose the way of life referred to as the single state for a variety of reasons. A consideration is that more women are finding fulfillment in careers that preclude the possibility of marriage in principle if not in practice. In addition to this work incentive, many young people today view critically, and somewhat apprehensively, the high divorce rate in the United States; they choose to avoid the psychological, emotional, and financial shock that accompany the disentegration of the marriage.

More and more the social stigma attached to being eligible but unmarried is passing; the single state is gaining acceptance in society. Furthermore, the high degree of mobility American business requires of its work force makes family ties less desirable to many men and women.

While these seem to be the dominant reasons why people choose freely to live in the single state, some people may choose this way of life because of their concern about overpopulation. Also to be remembered is the fact that since effective birth control methods have made sexual relations safer, singles can satisfy sexual desires without taking on the risks and responsibilities of marriage and parenthood.

II. Contemporary Theological Approaches

In the past, discussion of the single state centered on two points: First, a single person needed heroic virtue to observe sexual abstinence apart from the protection and support of a religious community; second, the single state required some sort of dedication to a particular work or vocation lest the person become selfish.

Contemporary approaches to this state of life include the following:

• Those living in the single state must not enter into any interpersonal relationship that could result in the arousal of physical, venereal pleasure. In other words, it is necessary for them to avoid persons who could be proximate occasions of sin.[1] The weakness of this approach lies in its failure to encourage the healthy interpersonal relationships that are essential to full human development.[2]

• Those living in the single state are free to live in any manner they see fit. They may engage in any form of sexual activity they desire so long as the individuals with whom they relate agree on the nature and limits of this activity. I refer to this as the consenting-adults approach. In practice it tends, more often than not, to promiscuity.[3]

• Those living in the single state must live in a manner that will contribute to their own growth and integration and that of others. This approach has the advantage of being equally applicable to all types of persons—married, single, and religious. The weakness lies in the fact that to live this philosophy involves a certain amount of risk and responsibility.

III. Lifestyles in the Single State

At this point we distinguish the major and lesser life forms within the single state and explain the similarities and differences among them.

A. Voluntary Singles

Every interpersonal relationship must be developed in the wholeness of one's personhood and therefore will be "sexual" in the sense that one relates to another in a manner that is distinctively male or female. The aim of every relationship should be mutual growth. Relationships that foster this growth are morally good; they attempt to reveal the depths of personhood. From this perspective superficiality and manipulation are morally repugnant.

A relationship between a single person and a married person of the same or opposite sex has the same characteristics as the relationship between two single persons, except that a three-fold relationship is necessarily involved inasmuch as the rights of the spouse are affected. Care must be taken to respect the third party who, understandably, may be hesitant to share in this relationship.[4]

What of the swinging singles phenomenon? This style of living, hardly new, involves a very casual approach to interpersonal sexual relations. The obvious danger is that one can become self-destructive, exploitative, and deceitful toward others, unstable, promiscuous, and consistently superficial. Sexual relations are too much a part of the person's core being to be used so casually.

Yet, it must be noted that relations between responsible persons need to include signs of human warmth and friendship, signs of love and affection. We are bodily beings who need to express our bodiliness in many ways.

While I would not condone genital intimacy, *per se* between two single people, I would say that an intimate expression of love between two honest friends of long-standing may be less immoral than the same intimate expression between a married couple who is selfish and self-serving, dishonest, and irresponsible! The fact of marriage should make a difference; too often it does not.[5]

B. Involuntary Singles

There have always been individuals in society who, for various reasons, have been unable to marry. All too often these individuals have been the objects of poor humor, ridicule, and social discrimination.

Involuntary singles would be better served if they were urged and helped to live their lives as true sexual human persons with the same needs, rights, and opportunities as other men and women. Such individuals cannot and should not be expected to live as

115

nonsexual beings. Rather, they can and must find true friendships that are enriching and not exploitative.

These persons have the right to signs of love and friendship proportionate to the depth of the relationship and the limitations of their condition. These are to be considered proper and appropriate so long as they demonstrate the healthy characteristics that should accompany all sexual interpersonal relationships.[6]

1. The Mentally Retarded The retarded are not rendered asexual by virtue of their condition, and are not to be denied the expression of their sexuality. Given special care and protection as well as special education and guidance, they can live as fully human persons.[7]

Taking into consideration their limited capabilities and the good of society as a whole, the retarded need to learn how to express the sexual dimension of their personhood so as to achieve that level of growth of which they are capable. They deserve education in sexuality according to their ability to learn. Parents, especially, should engender feelings that encourage the retarded person to experience their bodiliness as good and wholesome.

2. Widowed Singles The death of a spouse leaves the remaining partner with the options of finding a suitable second partner or facing life alone. Often society acts in a way that keeps a widow or widower alienated from the mainstream of society, especially married society. The need for healthy interpersonal relations, and the need for friends, both male and female, does not stop with the death of a spouse. Personal interrelatedness must be part of everyone's life regardless of age or condition.

It is interesting to note that women are outliving men at a higher ratio each year, increasing the number of older women, who as fully sexual human beings need compassion and love that is not readily available.[8]

C. Celibate and Virginal Sexuality

The ideal of celibacy and virginity has been an important part of the life of the church from earliest times. This mode of living the Christian life has been revered as a powerful sign of the mystery of Christian love, the eschatological hope for the second coming of the Lord, and the ultimate destiny to which every person is called.[9]

For celibates, as for everyone else, human sexuality is a great and good gift of God. Celibates are called to serve God and his people as sexual persons, not as people whose sexuality has somehow been neutralized or taken away. The love celibates bring to the world is profoundly qualified by their sexuality.

It is important to note that it is entirely appropriate and reasonable for Christians to choose approaches to life and sexuality other than marriage. It is a simple anthropological fact that many ways of living God's loving covenant are available to us. One lifetime can never actualize all the loving possibilities that God offers.

As valuable as marriage is, it is not absolutely necessary to the growth and development of every human person. One of the great cornerstones of our society is the notion of radical monotheism, a tenet holding that, in human affairs, there is only one absolute—God. Everything else in life is relative to that absolute.[10] Were we to say that marriage is absolute and that all other life states are inherently dehumanizing or unnatural, we would be absolutizing something other than God.

Every person needs to experience two major types of love. One of these is the love of mutuality, the love that is given in anticipation of a return from the beloved.[11] Married love obviously involves the beauty of mutuality, but so does celibate love, since celibates too need care and support from others.

The other major love is the love of liberation, a love that gives to the beloved without expecting a return.[12] Both married and celibate love need this dimension.

In marriage, while both loves are emphasized, the love of mutuality is more highly stressed than it is in celibacy. In celibacy, on the other hand, liberating love takes precedence. Here lies the distinctive quality of the celibate life. This liberating love must serve as a means of giving witness to faith in the resurrection of Jesus. The celibate lifestyle is thus a style of prophetic witness, a style that travels lightly and tries to set people free so that all might live more fully the common Christian hope in the second coming of Christ.[13]

IV. PREMARITAL SEXUALITY

We now turn our attention to the second aspect of our study, namely the role that sexual expression plays in the lives of the unmarried.

Because sexual behavior has social implications and meaning, no society has ever been completely indifferent to the sexual behavior of its members. In every known culture, both primitive and civilized, sexual activity has been regulated at least to a certain extent.[14] The usual methods employed by society to render sexual expression legitimate are marriage and the family unit.

A. Theological Overview

Based on the scriptural vision, one of the basic insights of moral theology has been the fact that an essential relationship exists between sex and marriage. But, in the evaluation of sexual mores, this relationship has not always been recognized as an absolute principle.[15]

Historically speaking, a number of essential values have been stressed with greater or lesser force over the centuries. Among these values are the social dimension of sexuality and the importance of fidelity and love within sexual relationships. Sexuality has always been considered essential to life and intrinsic to the dignity of the person. For such reasons Catholic theology has attempted to enshrine ultimate physical expression within the experience of marriage. It has viewed all forms of premarital intercourse as fornication, as a violation of personal dignity, as manipulation, and, hence, gravely sinful.[16]

By definition, fornication is the exercise of sexual intercourse with mutual consent between an unmarried man and an unmarried woman.[17] Saint Thomas Aquinas listed fornication among the sins that were against chastity. He did not consider it as a sin against nature.[18]

Historically no distinctions were drawn between the premarital intercourse of couples engaged to be married and the relations of those involved in a casual liaison. No distinctions were drawn between adults and teenagers, between people in love and those for whom sexual intercourse was merely a matter of gratification. All premarital intercourse was viewed as fornication and, as such, was considered intrinsically and gravely sinful because the enjoyment of any sexual pleasure outside of marriage was considered a mortal sin.

Until most recently, Catholic moral theologians were of the common opinion that all premarital sex was forbidden by the bible. Theologians such as Saint Alphonsus Liguori did not have the tools of critical, historical, biblical scholarship at their disposal. Thus Alphonsus taught, along with other theologians, that all premarital intercourse was expressly forbidden in the bible by means of divine positive law as indicated in Leviticus 19:29, Deuteronomy 23:17, and I Corinthians 6:9.[19]

Arthur Vermeersch, S.J. was the first Catholic moral theologian to recognize that the Old Testament does not contain a prohibition against premarital intercourse as such. He concluded that the bible prohibited premarital intercourse only indirectly.[20] In the same vein, Josef Fuchs, S.J. admitted that the New Testament cannot be cited simply as prohibiting all forms of premarital intercourse.[21]

Today, Catholic moralists recognize that in the New Testament there is no prohibition against premarital intercourse as such.[22] What is secure, however, is that the New Testament explicitly condemns completely unhampered sexual intercourse, especially with a prostitute. The New Testament does not address the situation of intercourse between a man and woman engaged to be married.

In the past, as we have indicated, Catholic moralists traditionally have viewed sex as intrinsically ordered toward procreation. Thus sexual activity had to be limited to the legitimate context of marriage, a context that preserved the welfare of children. For this reason both Saint Thomas and Saint Alphonsus opposed premarital intercourse in all forms. From the time of Saint Alphonsus to the present Catholic moralists have argued that premarital intercourse is always seriously sinful, in view of the natural law that requires children to be brought up properly within marriage and the family.[23]

But questions have since emerged: If premarital intercourse is sinful because it endangers the possible infant to be born, why is it sinful when there is no possibility of children? Even Vermeersch had to agree that Catholic moral theology was not able to produce clear and cogent *a priori* reasons for regarding premarital intercourse as always intrinsically evil and gravely sinful.[24]

Because this basic reason for prohibiting premarital sex had lost its persuasive power, other theological arguments were offered. Some contended that premarital intercourse raised the incidence of venereal disease and endangered psychic well being.[25] Others offered social arguments, namely that premarital intercourse jeopardized the mutual trust and fidelity needed in a subsequent marital union.[26] Still others argued that, to be meaningful, sexual relations required a mutual, total, and exclusive self-giving for life, and that this is only to be found in marriage. This symbolic argument maintained, and still holds, that physical self-giving is but the expression of personal self-giving and this can only take place in a lifelong shared existence, such as marriage.

Today sexual intercourse is no longer seen in terms of procreation only. At the same time modern methods of contraception serve to mitigate the danger of bearing children out of wedlock. Thus the occurrence of premarital intercourse is far more common. For many it is not a problem, but a fact of life.

B. Current Approaches to Premarital Intercourse

I distinguish five basic approaches to the morality of premarital intercourse. These general stances often do not appear along clear cut lines, but blend together.

The first approach maintains that all directly voluntary sexual pleasure outside of wedlock is grievously sinful. This viewpoint adheres quite strictly to a procreative concept of human sexuality. Even the smallest amount of pleasure is an enticement to indulgence, and this would be fatal to the human race. I would state that this is an extreme position that was tempered by the 1975 Vatican statement *Persona Humana*.[27]

The second approach states that every genital act outside the context of marriage is immoral. According to *Persona Humana* sexual intercourse finds its fullest meaning only in a stable marriage sustained by a conjugal contract that is guaranteed by society.[28]

While this attitude notes the societal implications of sexual intercourse it identifies and confuses the legal and moral spheres. It does not take into account that, in this imperfect and ambiguous world, the conjugal contract and civil recognition do not always guarantee a genuine mutual commitment.[29] This vision is too extrinsic and legal to serve as a moral norm for an expression of life that is primarily personal.

A third approach holds that premarital intercourse is wrong, but preceremonial intercourse might be moral. This attitude is based on a distinction between inner mutual consent, which is the existential basis of a marriage, and the external manifestation of this commitment. These two moments do not always coincide chronologically; we may, therefore find situations where the expression of sexual intimacy may be termed preceremonial.[30] Since we have already shown that marriage is a process, there may be a time when sexual intercourse becomes an appropriate expression of intention and commitment. This could be true for couples engaged to be married, or for those who, although mature enough to marry, may be prevented from marriage because of external reasons such as finishing graduate school, or medical internship, etc.[31]

120

Those advocating this position maintain that the restriction of sexual intercourse to marriage is the ideal, and engaged couples should strive toward the ideal. But this position also recognizes the fact, that the period of engagement involves a growing togetherness, a deepening of love, and a movement toward physical intimacy. This intimacy on the part of an engaged couple might be the expression of a commitment already being lived. From a pastoral viewpoint I would say that this situation is far more common than we think.

A fourth basic approach states that sexual intimacy may be an appropriate expression of the quality and depth of relationship, whether marriage is intended or not. The proponents of this view see moral norms as relative, and strongly defend the freedom of mature individuals to act in accordance with their own judgments and in the best interests of the parties involved.[32] This they do by setting aside the rule.

By way of criticism I might note that this attitude seems to place an undo emphasis on motivation as an ethical determinant. There is an exaggerated role given here to the freedom of the individual and a failure to see the virtue of fidelity as the bond of commitment expressed in the symbolic act of intercourse.

A fifth and final approach holds that sexual experience, including intercourse, is a natural human experience, apart from intimacy.[33] This view radically separates sexuality from its personal meaning. Christian moralists are unanimous in condemning this attitude as being depersonalizing, dehumanizing, and immoral.

C. Pastoral Reflections

In light of the complexity of this issue it seems rash to presume that a clear and unambiguous norm will provide a simple final solution.

Premarital intercourse is indeed a common and growing phenomenon. According to the classic study of Kinsey in 1952, during the age span of 16-25, between 64% and 90% of single males experienced intercourse.[34] The 1953 report for females suggested that between 20% and 50% of single women had experienced intercourse in the same age span.[35] These figures now seem archaic as the numbers are much higher today.[36]

The taboos of the past cannot meet the needs of today's young adults. While these standards are not necessarily wrong, the majority of persons today simply do not recognize and accept them on a conscious level.

We must remember that human moral behavior can never be reduced to black-and-white categories. One cannot expect the kind of reasoning used in mathematics or physics to demonstrate the principles and conclusions of ethics. Ethics and morality are concerned with values, goals, attitudinal orientations, and the complexity of human nature. Ethics involves dealing with the world of ambiguity and conflict. If there were ever a time when a "thou-shalt-not" approach to premarital sexuality was successful, that day is now over and gone. The blanket condemnation of all premarital sexual intimacy is simply no longer taken seriously by the majority of American Catholics.

As of 1973, only 45% of American Catholics believed that premarital sex was wrong.[37] Sexual intercourse between an engaged man and woman was approved by 43% of American Catholics.[38] And even among the clergy, support for the traditional absolute is eroding. While 80% of the priests in the United States still regard premarital intercourse as immoral, 25% of those who are 35 years of age and under and 19% of those who are between the ages of 36 and 45 do not object to premarital intercourse in certain circumstances.[39]

Without doubt the traditional moral code concerning premarital intercourse is inadequate, especially in its lack of distinctions among the ages, attitudes, and intentions of the people involved. The alternative need not be hedonism, moral relativism, or the surrender of human values, Christian ideals, or ethical norms. Fidelity, fairness, and respect for the dignity of the human person are fundamental and enduring aspects of the Christian ethical response to the revelation of God's love in Christ Jesus. These latter elements must be preserved in an authentic stance regarding premarital sex.

D. Some Suggestions

I would stress that sexual behavior for a Christian must be guided by the same values and norms as for all other human beings. In other words, the Christian should be opposed to promiscuity, manipulation, irresponsibility, and exploitation.

It must also be remembered that sexual intercourse is an expression of a person's whole being, the deepest core of his or her personality. The introduction of sexual intercourse into a relationship alters that relationship radically in that it calls for repetition. Thus, for intercourse to be honest, a commitment to the relationship is required as well as frequent physical presence to one's partner.

Sexual relations that do not represent the whole person, that do not have the possibility of being sustained in a lasting relationship, that do not express the reality of two people being there in an exclusive way for each other are simply forms of exploitation, at best a matter of casual play that is unworthy of the serious quality of sex. Such exploitation falls far short of the command of Christ and would be immoral and dehumanizing.

We cannot, as in the past, construct a scale by which to determine venial and mortal distinctions based on the degree of passion between two people. It is, for example, both superficial and unrealistic to say that any passionate kiss before marriage is always sinful, even for the engaged couple. Honest forms of intimacy must be determined by the age and maturity of the individuals and the serious possibility of marriage.

Premarital sexual morality is largely a matter of drawing honest and appropriate lines. Couples should recall the virtues affirmed in the bible and held over the centuries. Then, looking into their hearts, they should ask themselves whether or not these values are being affirmed in their relationships, whether or not these virtues are being lived.

Even in the wake of the sexual revolution I must maintain that marriage is the ideal context for the full human realization and self-communication that is involved in the sexual expression of love. It is the human capacity for responsibility and fidelity that makes marriage possible; it is the human inclination to infidelity that makes marriage necessary.

QUESTIONS FOR DISCUSSION

1. When we think of the single state, do we think of it as a vocational state of life?

2. Regarding celibacy, what are your thoughts as regards this discipline as a necessary prerequisite for ordination in the Western church?

3. Is there really a distinction between preceremonial and premarital intercourse?

4. Indicate some concrete areas that might help in the articulation of a coherent view of the engagement period.

5. Is sexual compatibility a necessary element before marriage?

13

An Inquiry Into Extramarital Relationships

No institution is more conservative than marriage because it lies at the heart of social organization. Yet, as we near the year 2,000, this basic social grouping seems to be foundering, even dying. Is there an underlying cause? Can we pinpoint, with any degree of certitude, the reasons behind the struggle?

Maybe the problem lies with marriage itself. This is the position of Professor John Snow of the Episcopal Divinity School of Cambridge in Massachusetts. He observes:

> What we are now experiencing in Western society and with a vengeance in many parts of the United States, is the disruption of the core institution of marriage, and what seems to be the changing patterns of marriage are, in reality, frantic, impulsive, futile attempts of this core institution to maintain its equilibrium—or even more frantic, impulsive and futile attempts to find a new equilibrium. What we are experiencing at present is chaos at the very center of society.[1]

I. BACKGROUND TO THE PROBLEM

Is there an underlying cause for the societal chaos that we experience? Perhaps the answer lies in the fact that among human beings all sense of meaning and purpose is founded in the experience and continuation of depth relationships. Any radical discontinuity that occurs in these relationships, regardless of the cause, results in at least the momentary loss of purpose. The rediscovery of this meaning depends upon the establishment of some new relationships that restore our links to the lost past, or create for us a new vision in the present.[2]

A. Technological Developments

From a sociological perspective there seems to be in the United States a history of disrupted relationships that has played an important role in the creation of a sense of meaninglessness. Briefly stated, this disruption can be seen as the result of three major developments over the last thirty years.

First, the increased mobility of the labor and management force in America has resulted in a mindless transiency that has caused the American middle class to be an essentially rootless, disenfranchised and powerless sector of society.[3]

Second, computer projections have revealed a squandering of resources that makes us aware of the radical finitude of life.[4] This raised ecological consciousness has had a devastating effect on the self image of the middle class.

Third, marriage has been affected by the development of effective methods of birth control and safer methods of abortion. The value of parenthood has come into question. What was once viewed as a blessing has become an option and a possible threat.[5]

B. The Effects upon Marriage

The above-cited developments affected the American marriage scene in four major areas.

Most significantly, these developments have helped to destroy the myth of the "one and only love," a myth which holds that two persons can and should totally fulfill all one another's needs including the need for intimate companionship.

Second, these developments have contributed to an attitude of familial egotism in our culture. The nuclear family has taken on an absolute priority, demanding all one's time, money, affections, and concern. The institution of marriage, American style, encourages selfishness, possessiveness, and exclusivity instead of sharing. The family has become a noxious shield against the reality of the Christian message.

Third, we no longer consider divorce as shameful or as a failure. As Jessie Bernard notes in *The Sex Game:*

> Plural marriage is more extensive in our society today than it is in societies that permit polygamy—the difference is that we have institutionalized plural marriage sequentially rather than contemporaneously.[6]

Fourth, we witness the destruction of the idea that there should be no sex outside of marriage, either before or during. Today premarital sex is tolerated and the extramarital scene is one that is gaining in popularity.[7]

C. The Effects upon Monogamy

These developments have affected the whole philosophical underpinning of the institution of marriage. Four major problem-making elements within our environment are mentioned here.

First, our eroticized environment, coupled with prosperity, mobility, and effective contraception, have made it more difficult to retain monogamy's monopoly on sex.

Second, we face a vast increase in the number of man-woman contacts after marriage with no guidelines beyond the fact that we are allowed only one spouse, one sex partner, and, thus, only one heterosexual relationship of any depth at all at one time.

Third, for many, traditional monogamy seems to be in trouble because it has failed to adjust to the possibility that marriages based on and judged by the satisfied interaction of two persons can, many years later, become unliveable. This idea is supported by even a quick glance at divorce statistics in the United States. In 1969 there were 660,000 divorces in the United States; in 1976 there were more than 1,000,000.[8]

Finally, traditional monogamy is considered by many to be in trouble because it has denied a voice and a role in society to a new and expanding segment of the population, namely the single, the divorced, and the widowed. The assumption that sexual fulfillment is intrinsically connected with a marriage license is being tested.[9]

II. The Question of Infidelity

We will now focus especially on the last of the above-mentioned factors, namely, infidelity and its assault upon monogamy and marriage. Today, as yesterday, the average person defines infidelity as committing adultery and fidelity as not committing adultery. In the world of today, however, it is no longer adequate to define infidelity merely as having sexual relations with someone other than one's spouse.

Brian Boylan, in his interesting study entitled *Infidelity,* offers a wider definition:

Unfaithfulness as it is actually practiced by married men and women is much more extensive and involved than simple adultery. In addition to sexual infidelity, there is emotional infidelity and psychological infidelity plus many lesser forms ....[10]

A more accurate definition of infidelity would hold that it occurs whenever a married person repeatedly looks outside the marriage for satisfaction of a need not fulfilled by the spouse. The central term here is need. I would say that it is the rare couple who can be all things to each other. The gratifications that people today have come to expect and even demand from a marriage are so varied that few partners can supply all of them. The absence or denial of just one such supposed "need" can send the deprived partner stumbling into infidelity. Thus it is imperative that couples distinguish between the primary and secondary needs within their relationships. When an honest evaluation reveals that most needs are not being met within a relationship this may lead to infidelity or the ultimate break-up of the marriage.

A. Factors Leading to Infidelity

What are some of the basic social forces and factors that lead to infidelity in any or all forms?

1. Variation of sexual partners   In some cases the sexual relationship of marriage becomes boring and routinized and the idea of a new sexual partner seems different and exciting. In other cases, the person may feel realistically that his or her partner is no longer sexually adequate.

2. Retaliation   If one partner in a marriage finds out that the other has had or is having an affair, the result may be the attitude of retaliation, of getting even. We note cases of alcoholics whose neglected spouses often engage in extramarital relationships leading to intercourse as a sign of retaliation or as a threat to bring the spouse back to sobriety.

3. Rebellion   Some people may feel that the monogamous nature of marriage places an unwarranted restriction on them and that through extramarital coitus they can show their independence both to their spouses and to others.

4. Emotional involvements   A person may feel that his or her personal needs are not being met in the marriage relationship, and as a result the individual may seek satisfaction from an outside partner. While such sexual interest may develop slowly from mutual interests, concerns, or projects, very often these friendships drift to the romantic and genital levels.

5. Influence of aging process   This seems to be especially true as regards women who may want to prove to themselves and others, including their husbands, that despite advancing age, they are still attractive females. While men are not exempt from the insecurities aging brings, women seem to be more susceptible to the hidden anxiety that comes with age. This problem can be compounded by the fact that women tend to blossom sexually in the post-childbearing years.

6. Hedonism   Some people enter into illicit sexual activity, not to prove anything, but simply because they feel sex is enjoyable and should not be restricted.

B. The Nature and Extent of Extramarital Relationships

From an empirical point of view, how widespread is infidelity? Both early and more recent studies put the incidence of occasional extramarital intercourse by married men in their samplings at between 50-75% (Ellis 1972; Kinsey 1948; Terman 1938). Kinsey reported in 1957 that 26% of white American women had had an affair by the age of 40. Such adventures outside of marriage tended, among women, to increase with age, most frequently occurring between the ages of 36-42. Men, on the other hand, tended to decrease such behavior with age (Harper 1961). Married women who are unfaithful were as active in pursuing extramarital affairs as were unfaithful men (Athanasiou 1970).[11]

How is the extramarital relationship viewed by society? According to Morton Hunt, a lifelong student of the institution of marriage, Americans, unlike Europeans, give little or no recognized social status to the practice of infidelity. In America the "affair" continues to be seen as cheating; it is illegal and punishable by heavy fines, and can serve as grounds for divorce. It is secretive, and thus isolated from the rest of one's life. Americans, by and large, do not have affairs that last for years, nor do they engage in a continuous series of minor liaisons. The pattern seems to be an occasional brief affair now and then, so that most couples, despite the prevalence of infidelity, spend most of their lives physically faithful to each other.[12]

One gets the strong impression that, among men, perhaps the majority of those who engage in affairs are not unhappy with their marriages or mates. A fair number seem to indicate that they are "happily" married. Only about one-third seek an extramarital relationship for neurotic reasons. Most of these men do not feel that the affair is in any way harmful.[13]

Yet, so-called sexual "prophets," like Robert T. Francoeur, see the situation in a different light. In his view there has been a new appraisal in America concerning extramarital affairs. In the past, the compulsiveness and possessiveness that dominated these affairs often thrust the parties into an escape mentality, and the frantic, romantic, and unrealistic pursuit of greener pastures elsewhere.

According to Francoeur, the affair used to be seen as a "prelude" to divorce and remarriage. It became an escape hatch from one monogamous marriage to another, and was forbidden by a society dedicated to the idea of lifelong monogamy.[14] Today, he contends, marital infidelity is becoming for more couples a "positive" element, an alternative to divorce that will increase in the future.[15] This view is further clarified by Raymond Lawrence, an Episcopalian priest and marriage advisor:

> Though extra-marital sex is not new, what is new with increasing evidence is that extra-marital sex may be openly and contractually integrated into a marriage with creative and positive results.[16]

Thus the affair now assumes the form of a satellite relationship that is subordinate to the primary marital relationship. Thus a more flexible monogamy would see the marriage relationship as primary but not exclusive, specific but not possessive.[17]

It seems to me that whether or not we choose to adopt the apocalyptic vision of infidelity as consciousness-expansion, one important keystone remains to be examined, namely, the mystery and definition of fidelity. It seems to me that the Christian theologian of today must evolve a more positive and fruitful understanding of fidelity in order to expose the potential harm and real shallowness of this so-called new wave vision of marriage.

Fidelity must be seen as a virtue that flows from the experience of authentic life-commitment and promise-making. Fidelity means faith in the other person, trust, dependence, reliance. Fidelity as a virtue opens new possibilities for intimacy by showing how two people can love each other with heart as well as body. This vision would stand as a counter-sign to the new wave vision of experimental marriage and trial relationships.

C. Variant Patterns in Marriage

Today we face a variety of living patterns that are being adopted by couples, patterns that do not fit into our classical understanding of marriage.

1. Free Sex   By definition this is a radical contradiction of the value of fidelity. It is a thinly veiled form of self-gratification that is offensive to true Christian interpersonalism and is devoid of the joy that characterizes good sexual relations.

2. Common Law   Marriage, with all its deep interpersonal meaning, has always been an object of social and communal meaning as well. Those forms of common-law living that represent a total rejection of social values would thus be morally objectionable. But equally deplorable are the laws and structures that make such activity necessary.[18]

3. Communal Living   In general, this term refers to a familial situation of life in which a variety of people, married or unmarried, live a communal life together and work toward a goal. We hear of various types of communes throughout our society. These groups seek to make all equal and to promote corporate ownership. They fail to uphold individuality and the need to choose the partner to whom one will be faithful.

4. Moral Evaluation   How do we evaluate such patterns as the above-mentioned, from a moral point of view? It seems that there are basically three approaches.

First, is the approach that states all variant marriage patterns are evil, regardless of circumstance, because they reject some basic marital factors.

The second approach states that variant marriage patterns depart to one degree or another from the Christian ideal of marriage, and, in most cases, these patterns are not to be tolerated. This approach seeks to establish a normative general guideline.

Third, is the approach that states variant marriage patterns are largely private matters. These patterns can be legitimated by the mature consent of the participants and are acceptable so long as nobody gets hurt. This approach appeals to quasi-absolute self-determination. It fails to appreciate the sacramentality of marriage.

In evaluating all of these patterns, a final word must be offered concerning adultery. How do we evaluate adultery? In examining an adulterous situation we have to see the effects of adultery on at least three people: the two marriage partners and the third party. It seems to me highly unlikely that there would ever be a situation where such activity could be considered morally good. In most cases of extramarital relationships the virtues of honesty and fidelity are rarely present. The entire world of extramarital liaisons contradicts the biblical concept of convenant fidelity, the very heart of commitment and human fulfillment.

QUESTIONS FOR DISCUSSION

1. In light of this issue of extra-marital relationships, analyze the virtue of fidelity. Is fidelity more than non-adultery?

2. What is your impression of the views of the new-sexologists who speak of multiple relationships?

3. Discuss the concept of friendships within a marriage relationship. How does one maintain a relationship on that level?

14

Homosexuality

Any study of human sexuality would be both inadequate and incomplete if it were to neglect the question of homosexuality. It is difficult to say anything about homosexuality that is not of a provisional nature, since sufficient research has yet to be done in the areas of psychology, sociology, and medicine, as well as in theology. Although the field of pastoral care has entered a stage of research, dialogue, and practice, there are more than a few questions still to be raised, false attitudes to be corrected, and injustices to be rectified.

At the very beginning it would be wise to distinguish the various types of homosexuals. First, is the covert homosexual. This person can be found in the full range of occupations in society, often passing as a heterosexual. He or she could very well be married, but seek to become engaged in extramarital homosexual experiences.[1] Second, the overt homosexual. This person does not resort to any pretense but openly relies on the homosexual community for sexual gratification.[2] Third, is the deprivation homosexual, who is ordinarily heterosexual but who turns to homosexual outlets when heterosexual ones are not available. This type of behavior often occurs in prisons, in the army, etc. Frequently it is a transitory experience for the person and does not necessarily point to any inversion of sexual preferences.[3] A fourth type is the latent homosexual. This person has a strong but poorly repressed homosexual tendency, which surfaces to conscious activity after a certain period of time.[4]

It can be noted that homosexual behavior is never the dominant sexual outlet in any human society or animal species.[5]

I. HOMOSEXUALITY: AN OVERVIEW

Homosexuality is generally considered by authors and researchers as either an illness, a lifestyle, or a criminal offense.

A. Lifestyle

Homosexuals, like heterosexuals, are characterized not by one but by many lifestyles. Today the homosexual community represents a subculture in our society whose lifestyle encompasses many activities beyond sexual ones.[6] A particular mode of dress and vocabulary, an attempt to provide a self-sufficient world, unifies people in this subculture.

1. Male Homosexuals   The behavioral characteristics of male homosexuals are highly influenced by their vulnerability to harrassment, censure, and persecution by society. At present, the typical homosexual is psychologically isolated from society, dependent upon other homosexuals for sexual expression, and ruled by a concealed yet complex system of social relations and obligations.[7]

Probably the most common misunderstanding of male homosexuals is reflected in the stereotypes that portray them as swishy, limp-wristed, effeminate "faggots," "fairies," etc. To be sure, some individuals fit these stereotypes, and within the gay crowd they are known as "queens."[8] But these men represent only a small portion of the homosexual population and are by no means admired by the rest. At the other extreme are those who make it a point to look overly masculine.

Male homosexuals generally have short term relationships, though some ties may be very intense. As each affair tends to be short, the homosexual frequently needs to find new partners. As a result, many homosexuals go "cruising" in search of partners or pick-ups. Important as this cruising style is for most homosexuals, such behavior is not unique to them. Female prostitutes and heterosexuals of both sexes who are looking for "one-night-stands" operate in much the same way.

As far as sexual behavior is concerned, male homosexuals do whatever is physically possible: kissing, petting, mutual genital stimulation followed by mutual masturbation or *fellatio*, and anal intercourse. Homosexuals claim that through anal intercourse they experience the same satisfaction as do heterosexuals who experience vaginal intercourse. They also risk the gamut of venereal diseases.[9] In fact, due to the amount of physical activity involved today, physicians report many cases of venereal diseases occurring in oral and anal areas.

2. Female Homosexuals   Much of what was mentioned about male homosexuals can be applied to females, but some distinctions are necessary. It must be noted that lesbians tend to form more lasting ties, operate in less differentiated subcultures, and are generally far less often detected and harrassed.[10] There is a much greater tendency among lesbians to pair off and live as couples in relative ease and stability. Often the partners assume roles.

Lesbian activities consist primarily in kissing, caresses, fondling and oral stimulation of the breasts, mutual masturbation, and *cunnilingus*. Often lesbian couples try to simulate vaginal or anal intercourse by using a dildo, an object that resembles a penis. Kinsey's studies revealed a higher incidence of orgasm among lesbians than among women in heterosexual unions. This is often attributed to the fact that women know their female anatomy better than men do.[11]

B. Homosexuality as an Illness

Psychologists and other professionals, basing their opinions on theoretical grounds and clinical experience, view homosexuals as either having suffered stunted psychosexual development or as having been conditioned to respond to inappropriate sexual objects.

1. Causes   There are two main theories to explain homosexuality as an illness:

a) Physical

—neurophysiological: Homosexual activity is due to malfunction in certain portions of the brain

—hormonal: Homosexual activity is due to an imbalance of male/female hormones

—genetic: Homosexual activity is due to inherited defects.

These theories have been postulated as the result of physical examinations, chromosome studies, and endocrine tests. But the results are ambiguous and, to date, there is no scientific agreement regarding these theories. Thus there is no uncontested thesis which proves that biological factors determine sexual object choice.[12]

This lack of evidence does not mean, however, that no evidence will be forthcoming. Many researchers remain convinced, as was Freud, that there is a genetic or constitutional predisposition toward homosexuality and that the life experiences of the individual serve either to reinforce or extinguish this.[13]

Another theory involves the concept of infantile bisexuality, namely, that at birth there are masculine and feminine elements in an individual based on hormonal factors. A steadily growing body of evidence indicates that behavior and anatomy are both influenced by the relative amounts of sex hormones present.[14]

b) Psychological

The pattern discovered among homosexuals essentially indicates the influence of a dominant, over-protective mother and a passive, often absent, father.[15] Without doubt, childhood experiences are important but what is specifically relevant to the cause of homosexuality is more difficult to pinpoint.

There are also several approaches toward treatment. One basic theory suggests that one should attempt to change the homosexual's orientation to a heterosexual orientation. Relatively few cures have been reported, and even fewer have been documented. Many homosexuals do not consider themselves to be abnormal or sick, and thus do not seek treatment. If they are forced to go for treatment, they easily play the game. Chances of a change in orientation are better if the person voluntarily submits to treatment.

C. Homosexuality as a Criminal Offense

The law seems to be quite arbitrary when it comes to homosexual behavior. Legal attitudes run the gamut from tolerance to extreme opposition. Many countries now have laws permitting homosexuality in private between consenting adults.[16] In general all countries have laws against the soliciting and abuse of the young. Sentences for these offences vary.

D. Gay Publicity

Changes appear to be taking place in the homosexual world as a result of the organized movement of gay people. Homosexual men and women no longer feel ashamed and have come out in the open. Organizations such as the Gay Liberation Front and the Gay Activist Alliance are much more open and forceful in their efforts to promote the cause of homosexuality than were private groups, such as the Mattachine Society. Members of Dignity, a group or organization of Roman Catholic cleric and lay homosexuals, wish to retain an active role within the church.[17]

The extreme position that has emerged amidst the shuffle is that gay is good, and even better than "straight" sexuality. It is presented by some as the solution to overpopulation and as the finest bloom of human friendship.[18]

II. HOMOSEXUALITY: A THEOLOGICAL ANALYSIS

Nowhere has homosexual activity been viewed with as much abhorrence as in the Judaeo-Christian West. The only adequate explanation for this profound animosity is the fact that homosexual behavior is viewed by the bible as "a crime worthy of death" (see Leviticus 18:22; 20:13) and as "a sin against nature" (see Romans 1:26).

There is no doubt that the Old Testament condemns homosexual practice with the utmost severity, but this condemnation must be situated within its proper historical context. The background can be found in Leviticus 18:22 (see 18:3) and 20:13 (see 18:24). The fundamental theme of the Code of Holiness given here is "not to defile oneself." This prohibition must be understood as a matter of cult.[19] The term "abomination" means something that is detested on strictly religious grounds, just as was the worship of strange idols or the eating of unclean food (see Deuteronomy 7:25; 27:15; II Kings 23:13 and also Leviticus 11).[20]

The Old Testament rejects the Canaanite practices of cultic intercourse (Deuteronomy 23:17-18). Homosexual activity between men is condemned as an abomination in the books of Leviticus, I and II Kings, and Deuteronomy because of its connection with the fertility rites of the Canaanites.[21] Homosexuality is here condemned because of its association with idolatry. This prohibition was extended to women in the Talmud. While these statements are not ethical judgments in and of themselves, homosexuality is considered as deformed, as deviate, as not in keeping with the Law.

Christian thinkers over the centuries have been influenced by famous stories such as Sodom and Gomorrah (Genesis 19) and Gibeah (Judges 19). Both stories deal with sexual violation, that is, rape.[22] In the Old Testament tradition there is no explicit identification of Sodom with homosexual practices (see Isaiah 1:10; Jeremiah 23:14; Ezekiel 16:49).

Jesus made no connection between Sodom and sexuality *per se* (see Matthew 10:14-15, 11:23-34; Luke 10:12, 17:29). In fact, Jesus made no reference to homosexual behavior. Only later in the New Testament tradition is any explicit connection made (see Jude

6:7 and II Peter 2:4, 6-10). We also note the sexual interpretation of the apocryphal writings of II Enoch and the Testament of the Twelve Patriarchs, although these had no real effect on the Talmud.[23]

Philo of Alexandria appears to have been the first author to connect Sodom explicitly with homosexual practices.[24] By the end of the first century A.D., the "sin of Sodom" had become widely identified among the Jews as referring to homosexual practices. This interpretation had an influence on the later New Testament writings such as Jude and II Peter. Other New Testament references to be considered are: I Corinthians 6:9-10, I Timothy 1:9-10, and Romans 1:18, 22-28.

In the references from I Corinthians and I Timothy, homosexual activities are listed with other vices. Confronted with a world of depravity and license, a world of dehumanization and degeneracy, a Greek-Jew like Saint Paul would be repelled by what he saw: pederasty, child-molesting, seduction, etc. In describing the chaotic moral climate of Graeco-Roman society Paul does not single out homosexuality in any particular way, nor does he give it any extra consideration.[25]

Without a doubt, Saint Paul considered homosexual acts to be perversions of the natural, divinely-instituted order of human nature and existence. In Romans 1:18, 22-28 the reference to homosexuality is almost parenthetic. It is not the principal consideration in this passage. Rather, homosexuality is used here as an illustration of the chaos that follows as the result of idolatry.[26] In other words, sexual confusion is a byproduct of idolatry. As a Greek-Jew, conditioned by the levitical law, Paul understandably rejected homosexual perversion, whether by men or women. He seemed to castigate those who deliberately chose homosexual over heterosexual relations. Obviously, he was unaware of the modern discovery of inversion. He considered all homosexual behavior as willed and deliberate, and so to him it was perverse.

Thus there seems to be no distinction made in the bible between deliberate perversion and indeliberate homosexual orientation.[27] Nevertheless, the lack of this distinction does not negate the almost universal sense of moral repugnance for homosexuality expressed by the Jewish people.

The Christian tradition basically extends the biblical lines already drawn. The Fathers of the Church were unwavering in their denunciation of homosexual behavior. Saint Augustine and Saint John Chrysostom were especially emphatic.[28] But the dominant influence on patristic thinking by far was not Saint Paul but the story of Sodom understood historically and interpreted sexually. The reinterpreted Sodom story also affected civil legislation, for example, the Code of Theodosius and the Code of Justinian, which prohibited all sodomistic practices under pain of death by fire.[29] These codes have had great influence, even to our own day. Severe penalties were necessary to protect the state from a possible vengeance of God similar to that which destroyed Sodom.

The church has often been accused of sustaining an unrelenting persecution of homosexuals, but a look at the historical documents shows that this was not the case. We see church legislation on homosexuality for the first time in the 4th century at the Synod of Elvira.[30] After this the condemnations were relatively few and sporadic. From time to time sodomy was denounced, but always in conjunction with other carnal sins. Homosexuals were rarely singled out for special hostility. Even the manuals of moral theology gave a minor place to homosexuality, describing it as sodomy and condemning it as gravely sinful.[31] Magisterial pronouncements were meager. Although the church did not conduct an unrelenting persecution of homosexuals, ideologically it did help to shape the cultural and civic abhorrence of homosexuality.

Saint Thomas lists sodomy, with masturbation and bestiality, as an unnatural vice.[32] The basic presupposition was that the pursuit of any sexual pleasure outside the procreative purpose is against both nature and reason.

Since the time of Thomas, the Thomists have considered these "unnatural" sins as more serious than fornication, incest, or adultery. The stoic concept of nature having a purpose, the association of venereal pleasure with sin, and the common assumption that reason must rule passion had taken hold of the medieval mind.

We note as well the evolution of a double standard. The penitential books, church legislation, and tradition in general had penalized with severity homosexual acts committed by men while virtually disregarding the offenses of women. The reason for this disparity seems to lie in the sexist androcentrism of the West and the almost idolatrous reverence for semen.[33]

The post-biblical tradition continued the blanket condemnation often without recognition of the historical origins of the scriptural references.

III. CURRENT APPROACHES TO THE MORALITY OF HOMOSEXUALITY

Today there are four basic positions on the morality of homosexuality. We list them here and offer our thoughts on each.

A. Homosexual Acts Are Intrinsically Evil

This position has been concretized in several recent publications. In the 1973 pastoral letter of the National Council of Catholic Bishops (N.C.C.B.), *Principles to Guide Confessors in the Question of Homosexuality,* we read: Homosexual acts are a grave transgression of the goals of human sexuality and of the human personality and are consequently contrary to the will of God.[34]

This approach is given a further emphasis in the 1975 Vatican statement *Persona Humana:*

> For according to the objective moral order, homosexual relations are acts which lack an essential and indispensable finality....Even Sacred Scripture attests to the fact that homosexual acts are intrinsically disordered and can, in no way, be approved of.[35]

But in the 1976 N.C.C.B. letter *To Live in Christ Jesus: A Pastoral Reflection on the Moral Life,* we see a greater sense of pastoral sensitivity evidenced by introducing the distinction between homosexual activity and homosexual orientation. As we read:

> Some persons find themselves through no fault of their own to have a homosexual orientation. Homosexuals, like everyone else, should not suffer from prejudice against their basic human rights. They have a right to respect, friendship and justice....Homosexual activity, however, as distinguished from homosexual orientation, is morally wrong.[36]

Thus while the homosexual condition is not condemned, the activities are. If one can change one's orientation, so be it. If one cannot, then that person is advised by the document to pray, to do penance, to sublimate, or to abstain. The basic assumption is that homosexual activity is always destructive of human personhood. This attitude considers homosexuality to be intrinsically evil by virtue of the fact of biological analysis. In other words, in homosexual activity there is an intrinsic frustration of biological finality.

B. Homosexual Acts Are Essentially Imperfect

This position is based on the notion that human sexuality has its proper meaning in terms of the love-union between male and female. Even though homosexual actions are wrong, not every form of homosexual expression or union is necessarily condemned as absolutely immoral.

This position states, reluctantly, that it might be necessary at times to accept homosexual expressions and faithful unions as being the lesser of two evils, the other evil being promiscuity. This compromise may be the only way some persons can find a degree of humanity.[37]

Pastorally, this approach presents the heterosexual union as the ideal. It seeks to do justice to the holistic vision of humanity by acknowledging the fact of limitation due to sin. But we must ask: If the ideal is utterly unrealizable and incompatible with one's personality structure, is it really an ideal? The weakness of this position lies in the fact that it cannot be imposed as an absolute.

C. Homosexual Acts Are to Be Evaluated Relationally

The thrust of this position is to judge the morality of a union in terms of the nature and quality of a relationship. According to this position, homosexual expressions are *per se* neutral and become either moral or immoral to the extent that they express or prevent love, mutuality, friendship, commitment, and humanization.[38] Human sexuality is viewed as a vehicle of human communication.

This approach fails to address the question of the procreative or life-giving element in human sexuality. The dimensions of mutual love, faithfulness, and caring, which we hope are present in a homosexual union, are the bare minimum. Is it enough just to be in love with and care for a partner? I think that a further life-giving dimension is also vitally necessary to sustain a relationship.

D. Homosexual Acts Are Essentially Good and Natural

This position, held by the Gay Liberation Movement, espouses the free choice of sexual expression. It uses personal experience as its philosophical basis. It then tries to promote a universal cause based on personal taste and desire. This approach does not do justice to the ethical question of obligation or rightness of an act or situation. This position, which uses a too narrow perspective to justify itself, is an over-simplification of the issue and should not be taken seriously.

IV. PASTORAL REFLECTIONS

Catholic tradition has consistently judged that all homosexual acts are against nature and therefore gravely sinful. Underlying this tradition are not only prescientific psysiology and unhistorical interpretation of scripture, but also the historically emphasized connection between sexuality and procreation. Only procreation, it is affirmed, justifies the enjoyment of sexual pleasure.

As I have already indicated, homosexuality has been revealed by scientific research to be a phenomenon of bewildering complexity. The homosexual condition can be said to be in and of itself morally neutral, although physiologically and phenomenologically it appears to be truncated or deformed.[39] So much for the condition. What about the actions of the irreversible homosexual?

Even with a sense of compassion, I do not think we can say that no homosexual acts are sinful. These very well may involve sin to either a greater or lesser extent, even in the case of a fixed inversion. But the morality of homosexual acts, like that of all human acts, must be determined by the principles of Christian ethics and moral theology. We must seek to integrate with our Christian faith and its ideals the data offered by science so as better to evaluate the moral status of homosexual acts. I therefore offer some reflections in this regard.

We ought to be aware of the complexity of the homosexual condition itself. Inversion is commonly defined as "the erotic, sexual attraction of a person towards members of the same sex and a nonattraction or even repugnance to the opposite sex."[40] But a definition cannot exhaust the many factors involved.

Anyone involved in pastoral care ought first to examine his or her own attitudes about homosexuality and deal with the prejudices or assumptions that may be present. What are some of these? The assumption that all homosexuals are child-molesters. That all male homosexuals are effeminate and all female homosexuals are masculine. That all homosexuals are promiscuous. That all a homosexual needs to overcome this problem is will power or a genital heterosexual experience. That professional psychiatric treatment or psychological counselling is a proven and effective remedy for every person who experiences the homosexual condition.

We should also keep in mind that homosexuals are aware of being a minority group. They have a sense of being different, alienated, derided, lonely, and without much self-esteem. This should help us to realize their need for support, friendship, community, and association.

Finally, homosexuals seek love, intimacy, and relationships as do heterosexuals. They strive for ideals. Can we deny the moral right of sexual expression to the homosexual whose inversion is irreversible and seemingly natural? Must all homosexuals seek continence as a way of life? Heterosexuals have the freedom to say yes or no to celibacy.

Regarding homosexual behavior, the CTSA report *Human Sexuality* states that the homosexual must be bound by the same norms as is the heterosexual, avoiding depersonalization, manipulation, and promiscuity, in relationships. In other words, according to this report, once a certain pattern of interpersonal behavior has emerged, the question must be raised: What values are being affirmed and what values are being denied in this relationship?

It seems to me that at base the CTSA report makes a hidden equation between homosexuality and heterosexuality. This stand tends to suggest that homosexuality is just another lifestyle and not a departure from the norm. Homosexuality is a variant lifestyle, to be sure, but it is also an imperfect expression of sexuality and as such cannot be judged on a par with heterosexuality. Thus more caution and concern ought to be exercised regarding homosexual acts.

Faced with the problem of promiscuity, a priest or counselor might be wise to recommend close, stable relationships between homosexuals as the lesser of two evils. Such friendships need not be seen as proximate occasions of sin.[41]

As far as the blessing of a gay union or homosexual marriage is concerned, it seems to be both inappropriate and misleading to describe a stable relationship between two homosexuals as a marriage. Anything suggesting a sacramental celebration of marriage in this case would be poor policy.[42]

In the light of unanswered questions regarding homosexuality, the historical questions concerning the scriptural prohibitions, and the diversity of theological attitudes, we must, in my opinion, permit a homosexual freedom of conscience and free access to the sacraments of penance and the eucharist.[43]

As far as continence is concerned, I do not think any person should be bound to fulfill the morally impossible. Absolute continence is ultimately a grace from God that is not given to all on demand. Thus the priest or counsellor should assist the homosexual to be creative and to integrate his or her sexual personality. Furthermore, church leaders should speak out for the civil rights and equal treatment of homosexuals so that unjust social conditions and job prejudice might end.

In conclusion, there is much that is uncertain and provisional about this subject. Much research needs to be done and much more pastoral experience needs to be accumulated before efficient and life-serving guidelines can be established.

Questions for Discussion

1. Given the different theories concerning the causes of homosexuality discuss the cause or causes that seem to be the most adequate to date.

2. What is your impression of the issue of homosexuality as it is treated in the Scriptures and Tradition of the Church?

3. From a pastoral point of view, discuss the ethics of compromise advocated in this chapter. Is this a workable theory?

4. Should the Church be involved in the promotion of Gay Rights? What of other groups and other rights?

15

A Medico-Theological Look at Abortion

The announcement "I am pregnant" usually signifies pride, excitement, and fulfillment. But sometimes these words express deep horror, embarrassment, and despair. Occasionally, the joy of that announcement gives way to anguish, occasioned by the intervention of an unexpected illness or the discovery of possible fetal abnormality.

The last decade has witnessed a sharp and heated debate over unwanted pregnancy which has been influenced by many factors. Of primary importance has been the claim of numerous women that restrictive abortion laws deprive them of their rights to self-determination in crucial matters such as reproduction. These women claim that these laws were based upon punitive Victorian attitudes which were socially discriminatory, and that these laws led to the extensive practice of illegal abortion with its high cost in suffering and death.

An increased psychological sophistication and awareness of the fragility of our social fabric has led to a deep concern over the fate of unwanted children. This has been coupled with the intensified ecological concern over the world population problem and the use of abortion as a method of fertility control in the Third World.

We have also come to a realization that with the combination of urbanization, female emancipation, and the ideal of the small family, childbearing has been increasingly postponed while sexual relations have increased. Along with this we see the development of medical techniques that have reduced the physical risks of abortions in early stages of pregnancy to less than the risks of normal childbearing.

Of no less concern has been the acknowledged decline in the perceived influence of religious bodies upon individual moral attitudes, and the question whether groups have the right to impose their moral attitudes on abortion on others who believe differently.

On January 22, 1973 the United States Supreme Court in two historic decisions—Roe vs. Wade and Doe vs. Bolton—struck down restrictive and moderate state abortion laws, placing the public policy discussion in a new context. [1]

We note here some interesting statistics that were recorded prior to the decision of the Supreme Court. On the average, 180,000 legal abortions were performed yearly in the United States; the illegal abortion figure ranged from 200,000 to 1,200,000. There were 500 abortion deaths yearly in the United States. [2]

I. HISTORICAL OVERVIEW

Present-day attitudes toward abortion have been influenced by centuries of thought and practice in the church and beyond.

A. Graeco-Roman World

In the centuries prior to the birth of Christ, it was fairly common to see laws protecting the fetus. The following codes all prohibited causing the death of an unborn child: Sumarian code (2000 B.C.), Assyrian code (1500 B.C.), the code of Hammurabi (1300 B.C.) and the Persian code (600 B.C.). [3]

In contrast to these codes, we have the Graeco-Roman context. According to both Plato and Aristotle, abortion could be employed for eugenic reasons, such as population control. [4] In Rome abortion was usually practiced among the upper classes. The declining years of the Empire saw a callousness about human life creep into the hearts of the people. yet by the second century A.D., harsh anti-abortion laws were enacted as part of a general reform. [5]

B. The Judaeo-Christian Insight

The virtual absence of references to abortion in the Old Testament and the profound respect among the ancient Hebrews for procreation as a gift of God suggest that abortion was not practiced to any large extent among them. The New Testament makes no explicit reference to abortion and therefore no express condemnation. What is condemned is the use of *pharmakeia* (see Galations 5:20; Revelations 9:20, 21:8, 20:15).[6]

In A.D. 100 the *Didache* made a distinction between destroying what had been conceived and expelling it.[7] By the end of the first century the Apostolic Fathers were speaking emphatically against abortion as being incompatible with the law of love.[8] This voice of condemnation continued with Clement of Alexandria, Minucius Felix, Jerome, Cyprian, Augustine, Basil, and John Chrysostom.[9] In A.D. 314 the Council of Ancyra condemned abortion, but reduced the penalty for women who aborted illegitimate children from lifetime excommunication to a 10-year excommunication.[10]

Suffice it to say that the early Fathers of the Church condemned abortion in general, especially in conjunction with fornication and adultery. But only Tertullian discussed the problem of therapeutic abortion to save the life of the mother.[11]

C. The Middle Ages

During the Middle Ages the problem of ensoulment plagued the thinkers of the church. First, how does the fetus receive a human soul? Two positions were proposed. Traducianism held that the soul is biologically transmitted from the parents; Creationism held that God immediately and directly creates each soul.[12]

Second, when does the fetus receive a human soul? Abortion at any stage of fetal development was gravely condemned, but once the fetus was formed and had received its rational soul the offense would become more serious. According to Augustine, the soul became present in the fetus at the time of "quickening."[13] According to Saint Thomas, the soul was not created at the time of conception but was later infused into the fetus.[14] Thus the destruction of a formed fetus would be homicide, but that of an unformed fetus would be quasi-homicide.

D. Legislation and Ecclesiastical Sanctions

The first legislation applying to the entire Western Church that incorporated the notion of delayed hominization or ensoulment came with the *Decretals* of Pope Gregory IX in 1234.[15] Between the 15th and 18th centuries some theologians began to allow the abortion of a non-animated fetus in order to save the mother.[16] In 1588 Sixtus V and in 1591 Gregory XIV condemned contraception and abortion of both animated and non-animated fetuses.

These condemnations were expressed in general terms and no mention was made of therapeutic abortion to save the life of the mother.[17] However, in 1869 Pius IX declared that every direct killing of a fetus at any time after fertilization would be given the equal punishment.[18] In 1917 the Code of Canon Law required baptism for all aborted fetuses.[19] Vatican Council II (see *Gaudium et Spes* par. 51) declared that the unborn fetus is a person at every stage of its development.

The 1976 N.C.C.B. statement *To Live in Christ Jesus* goes further as it addresses the problem within the context of the American political scene of legalized abortion:

> It is therefore ironic as it is tragic that, in a nation committed to human rights and dignity, the practice of legalized abortion is now widespread. Every human life is inviolable from its very beginning.[20]

E. Protestant Reflection

Attitudes within Protestantism have varied over the issue of abortion. For example, both Luther and Calvin were very strongly opposed to abortion. As a general rule, they tolerated it only in the case of saving the life of the mother.[21] However, several factors have caused a rethinking of the Protestant position. In the first place, the theological certainties that once called for firm Protestant opposition to nontherapeutic abortion have become less certain. Second, the abortion reform movement has drawn upon the themes that are of great importance to the Protestant tradition itself, especially the themes of self-determination and the relational control of a person over nature. Third, the various mainline Protestant communions have accepted religious pluralism as a fact of life.

II. THE MEDICAL PICTURE

Biological facts alone can never adequately justify moral judgments, yet they are important ingredients of such judgments and we need to bear this in mind in areas where there is scientific consensus.

A. Biomedical Consensus?

For the biologist, there is no evident answer to when human life begins; the process of life's creation appears as a continuum.[22] Once the fertilization of the egg has taken place, there is a continuum of development, making it difficult to justify with exactness and certitude any sharp breaks. Nevertheless, upon one fact there is unquestionable agreement: the fetal tissue is unique. Unlike any other tissue in a woman's body, this tissue has a unique chromosome composition and genetic make-up, differing from either parent.[23]

The fertilized egg (zygote) remains in the fallopian tube for about three days, continuously dividing. Having genetic information from both father and mother, the zygote, travels through the fallopian tube and within five to seven days reaches the uterus. About one week after fertilization, through a continuous process of cell division, there is a cluster of cells (blastocyst) which in about 75%-80% of the cases succeeds within another week in implanting itself in the wall of the uterus.

About two weeks after conception the implanted blastocyst is called an embryo. A rapid increase in organ differentiation begins and by the time of the sixth week of pregnancy, all of the internal organs of the human being are basically present. Within another two weeks (at the eighth week) the embryo has matured into what we call a fetus. It now matures and develops what is already present.[24]

Three stages of fetal development are important for the abortion question: 1) the first trimester (12 weeks); 2) the 20th week or current point of viability; 3) the 28th week or former point of viability.

B. Methods of Abortion

We indicate here five more common methods currently employed to effect an abortion. The first is the IUD and "morning after pill." These can be termed abortifacient in that there seems to be the prevention of implantation of the blastocyst. The second is dilation and curettage, commonly known as D&C, which involves a scraping of the uterine wall. The third is uterine aspiration, which is a vacuum suction that quickly empties the uterus of both fetus and placenta. It is not a risky procedure. In the fourth method, catheters are inserted into the uterus to stimulate contraction or to break the amniotic sac which causes the fetus to die as it is expelled.

The fifth method employed between the 10th and 24th weeks is the most drastic. In this method some of the amniotic fluid is withdrawn and replaced with concentrated saline solution that kills the fetus within a brief time and then causes contractions so that the fetus is expelled.

C. Indications for Abortion

What are some of the reasons by which persons justify abortion? We briefly mention five.

1. Non-Psychiatric Medical Risk Numerous conditions in the past were thought to justify abortion. Today, with improved prenatal care and new medical techniques, most of these conditions that earlier were thought to place the life of the mother and fetus in direct competition no longer do so. Some of these threatening conditions in the mother were cardio-vascular, gastro-intestinal, renal, and pulmonary.[25]

2. Psychiatric Risk Pregnancy can be a time of psychological crisis. Some of the variables involved—age, number and ages of present children, the attitude of the father, economic conditions, personal goals, and the marital status of the woman—do raise deep questions. At present, there is no clear agreement as to which psychiatric indications might warrant abortion.[26]

3. Suspected or Proven Abnormality of Fetus Because fetal abnormalities are numerous, anxieties over the possibility of one plague many women. The causes of congenital abnormality include RH blood factor, fetal overexposure to radiation, serious hereditary defects, the use of harmful drugs, exposure to Rubella during the first four weeks of pregnancy, and others.

Today, through the use of amniocentesis, chromosomal abnormalities can be known with certainty.[27] Other defects can be calculated in terms of probability. In either case, there is no medical judgment as such that can answer the moral question of whether or not to perform an abortion. Will the so-called probable defect prevent the fetus from enjoying a reasonably happy life?

4. Rape If the fetus is conceived through an act of violence, or is hated by the mother as an unjust intruder into her life, ought this child be born?

5. Eugenics Should defective people be allowed to bring children into the world if it is known that said offspring will also be defective?

D. Legal and Social Factors

In general, we can divide abortion laws into three categories:

1. Restrictive Laws of this nature were in effect in the majority of states in the United States prior to the Supreme Court action in 1973. Technically speaking, restrictive laws are still present in almost all of Latin America, India, and France, though enforcement is lax.

2. Moderate   This type of law, found in the Scandanavian countries, strives to allow more legal abortions where reasonable grounds exist, but it stops short of abortion on demand.

3. Permissive   Laws of this type exist in the Soviet Union, Japan, and most eastern European countries. The provisions of these laws vary. The 1973 Supreme Court decisions have placed the American situation within the permissive category. A closer look shows why.

a) *Roe vs. Wade* (regarding a restrictive Texas law)

Without directly attempting to answer the question of when the fetus becomes a human person, the Court affirmed that the state does have an important interest in protecting the health of the pregnant woman and that it has yet another important interest in protecting the potentiality of human life. According to the Supreme Court, these interests are separate and distinct.[28] By virtue of this decision the Supreme Court moved from a rigid position to a more permissive stance in terms of the needs and rights of the pregnant woman.

b) *Doe vs. Bolton* (regarding a liberal Georgia law)

While the Court emphasized the fact that a woman's right to an abortion is not absolute, and while permission was granted to the states to be restrictive in the last ten weeks of pregnancy, the net result was that prior to the level of viability we have abortion-on-demand without any required committee procedures.[29]

What have been the results of such a shift in legislation? First and foremost, the total number of abortions has increased dramatically. Illegal abortions have shown a marked decrease, but have not disappeared. Also, persons who choose abortion experience less social discrimination. It must be added that contraceptive practices have not increased in permissive abortion areas. In fact, many see abortion as just another possible method of contraception. Finally, there has been a growth in the concept of freedom of choice for women.

III. The Moral Debate

As with any issue of complexity, deep-seated feelings, and competing values, the abortion question has given rise to a moral debate. We shall describe the different approaches, but note well that many individuals may not fall into any one category.

A. The Right Wing

The clear expression of this side can be found in the words of Pope Paul VI contained in *Humanae Vitae:*

> We must once again declare that the direct interruption of the generative process already begun, and above all, directly willed and procured abortions, even if for therapeutic reasons, are to be absolutely excluded as licit means of regulating birth....[30]

The central issue for this group is the sancitity of human life. This is affirmed by a genetic interpretation that the conceptus, at whatever stage of development, is fully human life and is to be accorded all human rights and the protection of the law.[31] This position is also articulated by theologians such as Paul Ramsey, Dietrich Bonhoeffer, and Helmut Thielicke.[32]

Although the God-given inviolability of the conceptus at every stage is the central affirmation of this school of thought, these arguments are also offered:

• The principal mark of a just and compassionate society is its defense of the defenseless, its special concern for the weak and the powerless.[33] Of all the living beings involved in the contemplated abortion, it is only the fetus that cannot speak for itself and thus needs to be surrounded by special legal and moral protection.

• Both the physical and mental health of the mother are grounded in and best guarded by serious restrictions on abortion. Why? This group presents two arguments in favor of their position. First, where there are permissive laws, many women still seek out the criminal abortionist for reasons of secrecy and expediency. Second, the mental health of the woman suffers from the experience of continuous guilt after abortion, a signal of some subconscious violation of the natural order. I personally think these two arguments are weak. The stigma of abortion is less strong than it used to be, so recourse to criminal abortionists is decreasing. Also, one must distinguish between true guilt and guilt feelings.

• The moral health of the entire society is at stake. Many argue that permissiveness about abortion simply and decisively opens the door to an unimaginable range of moral horrors.[34] If we begin making judgments on the quality of life rather than committing outselves firmly to the protection of all life, what is to prevent the so-called quality from being decided by those in political power?

Still others within this camp hold that abortion is a rejection of a world-view advocated by the Christian gospel for 2,000 years, a world-view that puts before us the high vision of sacrifice, concern for the weak and defenseless, and a willingness to undergo redemptive suffering.

Note that the so-called right wing is not opposed to abortion under all circumstances. Rather, this group is opposed to the direct and willful taking of innocent life. The principle of double effect is brought to bear on those rare cases of abortion that would be termed licit, such as the removal of a cancer of the cervix or the removal of the fallopian tube in the case of an ectopic pregnancy.[35] When from a licit act there immediately follows two effects, one good and the other bad and the good outweighs the bad, it is licit to "intend the good and permit the evil."[36] But four conditions must be fulfilled: 1) the act itself must be morally good or at least neutral; 2) the evil effect cannot be a direct means to a good result; 3) the foreseen evil effect must not be intended or approved but only tolerated; and 4) the good effect must outweigh the bad.

This group thus argues in the form of a syllogism: human life is sacred and must never be directly and intentionally killed; the conceptus in all stages of development is human life; therefore the conceptus must never be directly or intentionally killed.

B. The Left Wing

The other end of the spectrum is abortion-on-demand. The force of the left wing argument is that no woman who sincerely desires an abortion should ever be refused.[37]

All related arguments converge upon one central affirmation: the woman's absolute right to control her own body and its reproductive processes. Other arguments include the following:

• A permissive abortion system is necessary to protect women's lives and health by making medically sound abortion available to anyone who wishes it.

• Abortion-on-demand will preserve the autonomy of the medical profession since there will no longer be a division between those doctors who will perform abortions and those who will not.

• To guarantee that only wanted children will be born, abortion-on-demand is necessary.

• An abortion-on-demand policy is necessary if women are to attain equal status in society, be accorded their full civil liberties, and be free from male domination. Compulsory pregnancy is a form of slavery.[38]

• Only a permissive abortion policy will avoid the social and racial discrimination that flourishes in every restrictive system.

C. The Justifiable Abortion Stance

Each wing of the abortion debate focuses upon a very significant value or right. The real ethical problem that emerges in each case stems from absolutizing one value at the expense of all the others. In effect, this removes the ambiguity of any particular decision, which would be an over-simplification of our moral experience. Most people experience the conflict and competition of relative rights. Theologically, the relativity of all rights and values is part of the radically monotheistic affirmation that only God is absolute.[39]

The posture of ethical responsibility finds the reasoning used by both wings to be unacceptable. Realistic decisions on abortion involve human beings immersed in widely varying patterns of social relationships. While two particular decisions may be identical in the sense that the fetus is destroyed in both cases, the moral meaning of these two decisions can differ, sometimes considerably, because of different intentions, situations, social conditions, etc.[40]

In short, any social policy should recognize that, in spite of certain common elements among abortion decisions, there is both uniqueness and moral tragedy involved in each one. If we say that each situation has its own unique quality, we do not mean to infer that general principles are useless. We do mean, however, that no absolute right or principle can automatically resolve complex human dilemmas.[41]

Throughout the debate, the humanity of the fetus remains as a difficult but crucial question. If we reflect on it, we note that there are three basic ways of viewing humanity:

• **Genetic**   The fixing of the genetic code renders the conceptus human and hence inviolable.[42]

• **Developmental**   The conceptus is rightly considered human life, but it has an increasing capacity for personal human existence.[43]

• **Social Consequences**   The humanity of the fetus depends upon the consequences of that decision for social policy.[44] In other words, from what point does the state have a legal obligation to protect the fetus?

The developmental view affirms that there is something unique given in conception and thereafter, a human life that deserves profound respect. But it is not personal human life until it gradually develops the capacities for personal interaction and response.

But the truth of the matter remains, there is an ambiguity involved in any abortion decision, regardless of one's view of the human.

IV. Concluding Reflections

The truth of the right wing position, I would say, lies in that pro-life bias which ought to inform and influence every abortion decision. Any destruction of fetal life is tragic and we ought not hide behind sterile, clinical language that describes abortion as the emptying of the uterine content, and thereby disguises the moral import. Whatever a woman may feel about the contents of her uterus, it is not just another piece of her tissue. It is a human being, potentially but not yet personally. Succinctly stated, abortion is not just another surgical procedure; nor is it murder: Abortion is abortion.[45]

A woman's right to self-determination is the central emphasis of the left wing. While this right ought not to be absolutized any more than fetal rights, we ought to affirm that God values the personhood of woman and her fulfillment just as he values unborn and newborn life. Granting the high place accorded to women's rights, if a woman is to have true freedom concerning abortion, there is need for a variety of options.[46]

A related but often overlooked consideration is the rights of the father of the fetus. Although some fathers (married as well as unmarried) may care little about the woman's situation, and although some appear untouched by the agonies of an abortion decision, it is hardly fair to generalize from this.

I also comment on the unwanted or wanted child. Ethically, the core question is whether or not the fetus receives its value exclusively from being wanted by other human beings. Even on a purely human level, it is hard to establish this, but when the issue is seen in the light of God's concerns for nascent life the answer is clear: The fetus has value quite apart from the attitudes of other human beings, including the parents.[47]

By way of summary I list values at stake in any abortion decision:

• The recognition of the right of each human being to the most basic conditions of life and to life itself.

• The protection of this right to live, especially by those who have cooperated with the creative love of God.

154

- The preservation of a correct understanding of motherhood.
- The ethical standard of the physician as one who protects and cares for human life and never becomes an agent of its destruction.

For the Christian conscience, the ambiguity about abortion remains. Freedom is not simply unencumbered autonomy. The vision of self-giving love, sacrifice, and care for the defenseless ought not to be lost in favor of a simple bias toward solutions that are more personally convenient and immediately rewarding.

QUESTIONS FOR DISCUSSION

1. Do you think that the careless view about human life in the Graeco-Roman world help to shape the strong, pro-life bias of the Church? Explain.

2. If you accept the idea that human life is a continuum, is there a particular point of non-human life? Also, does pro-life also affect our views toward the elderly?

3. What should be the pastoral practice of the Church as regards women who have experienced abortion and the Sacrament of Reconciliation?

4. If a strong anti-abortion stance is considered an ethical position that should not be legalized, is not the same also true for a strong pro-abortion stance? Reflect upon the inter-connection of the legal and moral spheres.

16

Recent Issues in Biomedicine

Our technological advances in the life sciences, especially recent discoveries in molecular biology, have theoretically made possible the redoing or reshaping of the human race. In this respect people now have tremendous power over human life. All we need is the further development of certain technological skills to transform theory into reality. Some of these skills are already available; others are on the horizon.

Today, more than ever before, we are faced with a genetic dilemma. Geneticist Theodosius Dobzhansky put the issue in perspective several years ago with the following words:

> If we enable the weak and the deformed to live and to propagate their kind, we face the prospect of a genetic twilight. But if we let them die or suffer when we can save or help them, we face the certainty of a moral twilight.[1]

I. THE GENETIC SPECTRUM

In an attempt to solve this dilemma, we have several choices. The only persons who would not recognize any of the possible options are those who advocate a defensive medicine which resists any conscious effort to modify the condition of the genetic pool. Persons who adopt this stance treat individual ailments rather than seeking more adequate solutions by studying the broad genetic picture. We now look at these options open to all who do not share the defensive attitude.

A. Negative Eugenics

This is an attempt to eliminate hereditary defects that have already occurred in individuals or to prevent those who carry defective genes from passing them on to their offspring. This result is achieved by means of genetic counselling, genetic screening, genetic therapy, and voluntary and involuntary sterilization.[2]

1. Genetic Counselling   Interest in eugenics and in the knowledge and techniques of genetics has been demonstrated by the hundreds of counselling units that operate mostly from a negative eugenic framework. In other words, their only goal is the prevention of genetically undesirable marriages and/or pregnancies.

Until a few years ago genetic counselling was confined almost exclusively to premarital situations. Genetic screening for the most widespread genetic diseases was strongly advised. Today, at least a thousand possible genetic defects are known.[3] A woman who is not pregnant can be given a probability assessment with regard to possible aberrations that might occur with pregnancy.

Recent years have brought about a general shift in this area of research due to discovery of new methods of reproduction and the access by millions of people to legal abortion. In 1955 it was discovered that the amniotic fluid contains the sex chromosomes of the fetal cell.[4] In 1966 a method of photographing and systematizing these chromosomes developed. A process called amniocentesis, which involves testing the amniotic fluid taken from the mother's womb between the 12th and 15th weeks of pregnancy, now makes possible the detection of about 70 genetic disorders, most of them serious ones.[5] Much genetic counselling has been associated with this procedure. In some cases it is used for fetal therapy. But when amniocentesis is used for genetic counselling, the purpose is usually to find out whether the fetus has any really grave disorders, with the implicit or explicit intention to abort, if such be the case.

Amniocentesis still presents a 1% to 2% risk of hurting the fetus and provoking irreparable damage or miscarriage through infection or trauma. With a majority of Catholic theologians, I concur that it would not be licit to terminate a pregnancy because of suspected genetic defects in the fetus.[6]

Amniocentesis can be justified if it is performed with a view toward fetal therapy. According to Bernard Haring, C.Ss.R., to rush into amniocentesis with abortion clearly in mind is a sign of "a manipulated public opinion."[7] In other words, a false hope that technology can obliterate all defects is created.

Some might maintain that the role of the genetic counsellor is to provide a certain amount of strictly neutral information.[8] I cannot agree with that, for then the tendency would be to treat patients as case numbers rather than as persons. I would affirm those counsellors who do not intrude on the consciences of their clients. However, the manner in which they give their information should make it clear that they do not consider their patient's decision a neutral one, but one that involves grave results.

A number of moral issues cluster around the central question of genetic counselling as such. Is it strictly therapeutic or does it have a eugenic aim? Is the counsellor neutral or not? What force can a counsellor bring to bear on a couple?

2. Genetic Screening   With genetic screening, the focus shifts from the individual couple to the testing of whole groups of persons to determine the actual presence or carriers of a genetic disease. Recent screening programs initiated to detect sickle-cell anemia, Tay-sachs, and PKU have raised important new questions for medical ethics.[9]

The goals of genetic screening are as follows:

a) To discover early certain genetic diseases for which there exists effective therapy, and to direct the afflicted person to medical help. There is a problem, however, in the discovery of those diseases for which there is no effective therapy available.

b) To detect persons who are carriers of a disease and to assist them in making informed decisions about whether or not to have children.

c) To alleviate many anxieties.

The subjects of a screening program need various forms of protection. In the present state of genetic knowledge, it seems wise that mass screening programs be voluntary and that written expression of free consent be required of each participant.[10] Furthermore, the rights of privacy of each individual should be guarded.

3. Genetic Therapy   Genetic therapy is part of a broad field of genetic medicine that involves the diagnosis, prevention, and treatment of hereditary diseases. It is a new approach based on the assumption that people may attain the power directly to manipulate their genes for their own improvement.[11] It is referred to as genetic surgery when parts are removed or replaced, and genetic engineering when modification of genes or gene activity is undertaken so as to eliminate genetic disorders.[12]

Gene therapy differs from eugenics which makes no attempt directly to change the gene itself but tries to improve the quality of the human gene pool by improving the environment and the total human condition. It differs from positive genetic engineering in that in the latter the patient is the whole human race, whereas

158

genetic therapy treats the individual living patient at the beginning of his or her existence.

The new type of gene therapy advocated today attacks deleterious genes surgically, by chemical means, or by means of radiation so as to reverse a mutation or to eliminate wrong genetic information in the DNA.

The techniques of genetic therapy differ according to the main forms of genetic disorders.[13] There are diseases with a variety of causes: aberration in the number of chromosomes, gene mutation, gene interaction, maternal-fetal blood incompatibility.

What are some alternatives to these problems offered today by scientists and geneticists? Basically these are reduced to four: These alternatives cover the spectrum from doing nothing to radical alteration.

a) Stop treating serious genetic disorders and let natural selection take control again. This is an unacceptable position.

b) Treat individuals, but block the further pollution of the gene pool by means of contraception, sterilization, and restrictive marriage licenses for carriers of gravely defective genes.

c) Allow people who have genetic defects to marry and reproduce, but determine by amniocentesis whether or not each pregnancy would be brought to term.

d) Treat genetic disorders in every way other than by direct gene therapy: diets, supply of missing vitamin and mineral elements, immunology, enzyme inducement, surgery.

B. Positive Eugenics

This is concerned with improving the race through various forms of controlled reproduction such as AID, artificial inovulation, *in vitro* fertilization, and selected cloning.[14]

1. Fertilization *in Vitro*   Artificial insemination, in the strictest sense of the term, is now a fact by virtue of the birth of several famous test-tube babies.[15] Fertilization of the ovum and the development of the germinal cell through the initial stages of life occur outside the mother, with the intention of eventual implantation in the womb.

Those who hold "ensoulment" at the moment of fertilization will be forced to refer to this procedure as immoral, especially if it must be interrupted at a certain stage. In their eyes, this would be homicide. I do not share this viewpoint. Rather, if at the present stage of embryological science we give a high probability to the option that individuation does not coincide with fertilization, but that hominization in the full sense happens at a later stage, then experimentation at initial cell stages cannot be termed homicide.[16] The element of risk, however, must be reduced insofar as possible. The psychic and physical health of the mother must be safeguarded.

2. Artificial Inovulation   This term refers to the artificial insertion of an egg into a woman's uterus or fallopian tube. From a technical point of view, it is possible to remove a fertilized egg from one woman's body and transplant it in a foster mother, who then carries the baby to term.[17]

The combination of test-tube fertilization with artificial inovulation could be employed for the woman who is not sterile and yet cannot conceive because of malformed oviducts. This condition is a major cause of infertility. Such a woman's unfertilized egg might be removed, fertilized with the husband's sperm *in vitro* and then the embryo would be implanted in the womb.

There are differences between this procedure and AIH. With AIH the actual conception takes place within a woman's body, but in artificial inovulation both fertilization and the early stages of embryonic development take place in a laboratory.[18] We must ask: Is test-tube fertilization wrong simply because it occurs in a test-tube?

A further question emerges: What is the moral evaluation of disposing fertilized eggs that are not used? Scientifically, in order to maximize the chances of one successful implantation, eight to ten eggs have to be fertilized. Those who believe that human life in its fullness begins at the moment of conception would see this process as morally repugnant. If, however, one holds, as I do, a developmental view, that sees human life as a continuum of growth that cannot be divided neatly into stages, these disposed eggs do have moral value, although this value would be less than that of the fetus. Although there is a certain moral ambiguity surrounding their deaths, their value may be far outweighed by the value of the potential child.[19] Another question arises: What of the genetic risk to the embryo implant? This procedure is not free of risks and there are no complete data as yet. Even with natural procreation there are risks.

Thus, we might observe two arguments that are brought forth. 1) The position that is in opposition to the pro-natalist view, which maintains that a couple has the right to be fertile by any means possible,[20] states that there is no absolute right to fertility. 2) The wedge argument, maintains that once accepted for therapeutic reasons this approach can be used for any reason what-soever.[21]

I would say that fear of the presumed large-scale moral horrors that could follow upon *in vitro* fertilization is not in itself a persuasive argument in general against the procedure. The potential abuse of something ought not to preclude its justifiable use, unless those abuses are deemed to be necessarily involved and unavoidable in the use of a procedure. Yet, the genetic risks to the potential child are great enough for me to offer a negative response to this procedure at this time.

3. Ectogenesis This is a procedure of artificial pregnancy from fertilization to birth. This involves a complete dehumanization of procreation. It seems to suggest an unethical level of experimentation with human beings solely for the sake of reshaping the species. The risks here are very high. The psychological trauma that could be caused for a fetus bred outside the human milieu without the essential symbiotic mother-child relationship would be devastating.[22]

4. Foster Womb With this procedure, a woman in whom the fertilized egg is implanted from someone else would be a host mother. She offers her womb as a foster home. In doing so she may be acting as a mercenary or she may be motivated by generosity.[23]

There is a great variety of situations that might present themselves in this regard. For example, a healthy woman might not want to jeopardize her career because of the inconvenience of a pregnancy. Or a woman might want a child but she might be anguished over the thought of pregnancy. Also, the health of the woman might not warrant a pregnancy. Some couples experiencing such a problem might seek a foster mother in whom would be implanted the blastocyst gained through *in vitro* fertilization of the sperm and ovule of the couple desiring the child.

We must admit that in terms of chromosomal damage there is a health risk to the embryo in the process of implantation. A further objection can be raised from a psychological point of view: The problem of mother-fetus attachment might lead to a later problem in the parent-child relationship.

5. Egg Graft This is a mirror image of AID, for now it is the woman who is sterile. She receives a ripe egg from an anonymous donor. The egg is implanted in one of her fallopian tubes and there it is fertilized by her husband through normal intercourse. The implantation procedure is risky and warrants grave caution.[24]

161

6. Artificial placenta   When medically indicated, a fetus can be removed from the mother's womb as early as 25 weeks after conception and safely raised in an incubator.[25] Hopeful attempts are now being made to keep alive human fetuses expelled by miscarriages as early as 10 weeks after conception. There are weighty advantages to having a placenta-lined incubator. When one is constructed, an interruption of a pregnancy due to grave therapeutic indications would no longer necessarily be an abortion but a transplant of the fetus into a glass womb.[26]

C. Genetic Engineering: Asexual Reproduction

Methods are now being developed whereby human reproduction can be achieved by means other than sexual intercourse.

1. Monogenesis   This phenomenon, known as parthenogenesis or virgin birth, can happen as a natural event.[27] It happens in frogs, rabbits, and turkeys, and it cannot be absolutely *a priori* excluded in humans. To date no reason for this occurrence has been discovered. What has been observed in animals is induced monogenesis caused by chemical or electrical stimulation or shock.

2. Cloning   According to the theory, the nucleus of an unfertilized egg is removed by microsurgery or irradiation and is replaced by the nucleus of an asexual cell of a male or female adult organism, usually an intestinal or skin cell. For reasons not yet known, the egg, with its implanted nucleus, develops as if it had been fertilized by sperm.[28]

The gene in these cases is determined only by the donor of the nucleus. If the nucleus was taken from a cell of the woman whose egg is activated, then her child will be her identical twin. If the nucleus is taken from the cell of a husband or donor, then the child will be the twin or double of the husband or donor whose cell nucleus activates the egg. Thus one person could be the sole parent of his or her duplicate. Sex choice also becomes possible.[29]

Scientists have all the clues for cloning. It has been successful with frogs but only after a large number of mutations. Thus once again we must fully consider and discuss the far-reaching implications of this procedure. I hope scientists will not try cloning human beings until the hazards are eliminated by successful experiments in cloning animals.

Cloning represents totally bypassing the physical sexual relationship. It represents the complete split between the unitive and procreative aspects of sexuality. This would have profound effects on all human relationships. For example, what would its effect be on a new generation and its need for identity, for belonging, for continuity, and the willingness to accept commitment?

What we have here is depersonalization in its most extreme form, namely, the abolition of human personhood and incarnate subjectivity. Furthermore, cloning would undermine the stability of marriage and family, for it would destroy trust, belonging, and acceptance. A real problem emerges when we have one group manufacturing another group. Who is to decide on the types to clone? What kind of humanity do we seek? The strong? The intelligent? The compassionate? The humble?

II. ETHICAL REFLECTIONS

One can succinctly say, after reviewing the most recent literature, that a new scientific determinism has emerged, especially in the United States. It is based on a technocratic logic that assumes that those things that can be done will be done and should be done. Connected with this determinism, however, is the strange assumption of utter freedom, freedom for the scientific manipulation of creaturely life.[30]

From a Christian perspective, I would maintain that we are not fated to do everything genetically that we now have or will soon have the power to do. Nor are we utterly free to manipulate our human future. We need to see both sides. Too great a certitude about inviolable human rights can result in an individualism that gazes fixedly upon the present with insufficient sensitivity to the changing needs of the human community. There is a relativity and a historicity about our notions of human rights that make them less than absolute.[31] On the other hand, those who act with undue confidence in judging certain scientific policies simply by the amount of social good they can produce may well ride roughshod over individual rights and human values in their eagerness to achieve those social goods.

With our present state of genetic knowledge, our focus ought to be on the area of negative eugenics, the elimination of specific defects in specific patients. But we cannot absolutely preclude the possibility that some day certain positive eugenic measures might be warranted both by the condition of the genetic pool and by increased scientific understanding. What is needed, I believe, is a concentrated attention given to public policy.[32]

A hopeful Christian realism about human life can go far in counteracting the extremes of technological utopias and nightmarish doomsdays which now creep into the discussions about genetics. A hopeful Christian vision of what makes human life truly human will encourage those genetic efforts which, even now, are relieving much suffering and contributing much to human wholeness. On the other hand, a wise Christian realism will challenge the biological engineers who are not content with humankind but are ambitiously intent upon improving the race. With all due respect to their achievements, I believe that salvation lies beyond any human evolution and that any human movement which claims ultimacy for its own vision breeds tragedy. This is the posture of hopeful realism that I would advise in this realm.

QUESTIONS FOR DISCUSSION

1. Discuss the differences between positive and negative eugenics. Is there a qualitative difference between the two?

2. In view of the therapeutic value that can be gleaned by the use of amniocentesis, should this test ever be employed as a prelude to abortion? What about a means of determining sex?

3. In terms of the so-called artificial means of inducing life, what do you feel should be the responsibility of the scientist? What about the mistakes that take place?

4. In light of the advances in science and technology we have been forced to re-examine and possibly re-define what it means to be human. Discuss the ingredients that make a human being to be a human being.

Notes

Introduction

1. Some of these handbooks are the following: J.C. Ford and G. Kelly, *Contemporary Moral Theology, Vols. I & II* (Westminster, MD: Newman Press, 1959); B.H. Merkelbach, *Summa theologiae moralis ad mentem D. Thomae et ad normam iuris novi, Vol. II* (Paris: Desclee de Brouwer, 1938); M. Zalba, S.J., *Theologiae moralis summa* (Madrid: BAC, 1957).
2. One book that certainly symbolizes this vision is Michael Volente, *Sex: The Radical View of a Catholic Theologian* (New York: Bruce, 1970).
3. This shift is characterized by a movement from metaphysics to epistemology. The point of departure for human meaning has shifted from questions of causality to questions of significance. This is not to deny causality but rather to place the perspective of human inquiry within the historical plane of meaning.
4. See David Tracy, *The Achievement of Bernard Lonergan* (New York: Herder & Herder, 1970), pp. 82-103.
5. Andrew Greeley, *Sexual Intimacy* (Chicago: Thomas More, 1973), p. 35.

CHAPTER 1

1. William E. Masters and Virginia E. Johnston, *Human Sexual Response* (Boston: Little, Brown, 1966) and *Human Sexual Inadequacy* (Boston: Little, Brown, 1970).
2. Peter Whittaker, *The American Way of Sex* (New York: G.P. Putnam's Sons, 1974).
3. L.R. O'Connor, *Photographic Manual of Sexual Intercourse* (New York: Pent-R Books, 1969), p. 44.
4. Theodore Roszak, *The Making of a Counter-Culture* (Garden City, New York: Doubleday, 1969), p. 15.
5. Eugene Kennedy, *The New Sexuality: Myths, Fables and Hang-ups* (Garden City, New York: Doubleday, 1972), pp. 118-119.
6. See Michael Leach, *"I Know It when I See It": Pornography, Violence, and Public Sensitivity* (Philadelphia: Westminster, 1975), p. 16.
7. Leach, p. 16.
8. Leach, p. 16.
9. See Jack Dominion, "A Word About Pornography" in *Sex: Thoughts for Contemporary Christians,* edited by Michael Taylor, S.J. (New York: Doubleday, 1972), p. 192.
10. See John R. Cavanaugh, *Sexual Anomalies and Counseling* (Washington, D.C.: Corpus Books, 1969).
11. See Kennedy, *New Sexuality,* p. 121.

CHAPTER 2

1. See Donald Goergen, *The Sexual Celibate* (New York: Seabury, 1974), p. 51.
2. See Robert Francoeur, *Utopian Motherhood* (New York: Doubleday, 1970), pp. 221-264.
3. To follow this development in the thought of Erikson see: Erik Erikson, *Identity: Youth, and Crisis* (New York: W.W. Norton, 1965), p. 94. See also Erikson, *Childhood and Society* (New York: W.W. Norton, 1966), p. 273.
4. Erikson calls this *ego-integrity* which is the truth of a person. See *Identity,* p. 139.
5. This is the crisis of intimacy vs. isolation. Here intimacy means a readiness for mutuality. See Erikson, *Childhood,* p. 263.
6. Abraham Maslow, *Motivation and Personality: Religion, Values, and Peak Experiences* (New York: Harper & Row, 1970), p. 23.
7. Maslow, p. 23.
8. Rollo May, *Love and Will* (New York: W.W. Norton, 1969), p. 311.
9. Maslow, pp. 105-107.
10. See Goergen, *Sexual Celibate,* p. 64.
11. Richard Stoller, *Sex and Gender* (New York: Science House, 1968), pp. 39-64.
12. Goergen, *Sexual Celibate,* p. 64.
13. See Goergen, p. 66.
14. See Stoller, *Sex and Gender,* p. 29.
15. We recall the enlightening thoughts of the scientist-theologian-poet Teilhard deChardin on this point.
16. Goergen, *Sexual Celibate,* p. 68.
17. See Jeanne Humphrey Block, "Conceptions of Sex Role: Some Cross-Cultural and Longitudinal Perspectives," *American Psychologist,* 28 (1973), p. 512.
18. Stoller, *Sex and Gender,* p. 3-23; 65-85; 262-68.
19. See Charles N. Cofer, *Motivation and Emotion* (Glenview, IL: Scott, Lawson, 1972), pp. 48-57.
20. See Goergen, *Sexual Celibate,* p. 75.
21. See Anthony Kosnik, *et al., Human Sexuality: New Directions in American Catholic Thought* (New York: Paulist Press, 1977). On this point it is interesting to read the sobering critique of George T. Montague, "A Scriptural Response to the Report on Human Sexuality," *America* (Oct. 29, 1977), pp. 284ff.
22. While the authors of the CTSA report agree with this statement they do not support it from the text.
23. See Bruce Birch and Larry Rasmussen, *Bible and Ethics in the Christian Life* (Minneapolis: Augsburg, House, 1976). See also Timothy O'Connell, *Principles for a Catholic Morality* (New York: Seabury, 1978), p. 20.
24. See Andre Guindon, *The Sexual Language* (Ottawa: University of Ottawa Press, 1977), p. 34.

25. Sacred Congregation for the Doctrine of the Faith, *Persona Humana: Declaration on Sexual Ethics* (Washington, D.C.: U.S.C.C., 1977), n.1, p. 3.
26. See Philip Keane, S.S., *Sexual Morality: A Catholic Perspective* (New York: Paulist Press, 1977), p. 15.
27. Guindon, *Sexual Language*, p. 47.
28. Pierre Grelot, *Man and Wife in Scripture*. Translated by Rosaleen Brennan (London: Burns & Oates, 1964), pp. 14-39.
29. See Edouard Schillebeeckx, O.P., *Marriage: Human Reality and Saving Mystery, Vol. I*, translated by N.D. Smith (New York: Sheed & Ward, 1965), pp. 14-15.
30. Gerhard von Rad, *Old Testament Theology, Vol. I*, translated by D.N.G. Stalker (Edinburgh: Oliver & Boyd, 1967), pp. 27-28.
31. May, "Sexuality and Fidelity in Marriage," p. 278.
32. Bernard Haring, C.Ss.R., *Free and Faithful in Christ, Vol. II* (New York: Seabury, 1979), pp. 494-497.
33. See Kosnik, *et al., Human Sexuality*, p. 83.
34. See William May, "Sexuality and Fidelity in Marriage," *Communio* (Fall 1978), pp. 276-277.
35. See William Luijpen, *Existential Phenomenology* (Pittsburgh: Duquesne University Press, 1969), pp. 311-312.
36. See Goergen, *Sexual Celibate*, pp. 31-33.
37. For the biblical concept of *sarx* see Xavier Leon-Dufour, "Flesh" in *Dictionary of the Bible*, edited by Xavier Leon-Dufour (New York: Seabury, 1975), pp. 185-188.
38. Dufour, p. 188.
39. See Haring, *Free and Faithful*, p. 494.
40. *Codex Iuris Canonici* (Typis Polyglottis Vaticanis, MCMLXV), canon 1013, n.1, p. 281.
41. Vatican Council II, *Gaudium et Spes* in *Enchiridion Vaticanum* (9th ed.), (Bologna: Edizioni Dehoniane, 1971), par. 49.
42. National Committee for Human Sexuality Education, *Education in Human Sexuality for Christians* (Washington, D.C., 1981).

CHAPTER 3

1. *Gaudium et Spes,* par. 41.
2. The ideas in this section were first recorded in my book, *To Live in Christ: Reflections on Christian Moral Life* (Palm Springs, FL: Sunday Publishers, 1979), p. 37.
3. Vatican Council II, *Declaration on Religious Freedom* in *Enchiridion Vaticanum,* 9th ed. (Bologna: Edizioni Dehoniane, 1971), #3.
4. See Josef Fuchs, S.J., *Human Values and Christian Morality* (Dublin: Gill & McMillan, 1970), p. 95.
5. See Thomas Garrett S.J., *Problems and Perspectives in Ethics* (New York: Sheed & Ward, 1969), p. 95-96.

6. The ideas in this section were first presented by me in *To Live in Christ,* p. 29.
7. See Fuchs, *Human Values,* p. 93.
8. Fuchs, p. 93.
9. Josef Fuchs, S.J., "The Absoluteness of Moral Terms," *Gregorianum,* 52 (1971), p. 271.
10. Avvento, *To Live in Christ,* p. 30.
11. Avvento, p. 30.
12. See Kosnik, *et al, Human Sexuality,* p. 82.
13. *Gaudium et Spes,* par. 10.
14. Sacred Congregation for the Doctrinen of the Faith, *Persona Humana* (Washington, D.C., U.S.C.C., 1977).
15. See Louis Janssens, "Ontic Evil and Moral Evil," *Louvain Studies,* 4 (1972).
16. See Janssens.
17. Fuchs, *Human Values,* p. 97.
18. See Richard McCormick, S.J., *Ambiguity in Moral Choice* (Marquette: Marquette University Press, 1974), pp. 116-117.
19. McCormick, p. 117.
20. Franz Bockle, *Fundamental Concepts of Moral Theology.* (Paramus, NJ: Paulist Press, 1970), p. 51.
21. Fuchs, "The Absoluteness of Moral Terms," p. 360.
22. Kosnik, *et al., Human Sexuality,* p. 91.
23. Jerome Lejeune, "The Instincts of Love," in *Commentaries on the Vatican Declaration on Sexual Ethics* (Washington, D.C.: U.S.C.C., 1976), pp. 67-69.
24. See *Gaudium et Spes,* par. 49. Cf. *Persona Humana,* n. 11.
25. See Haring, *Free and Faithful, Vol. II,* p. 310.
26. See Richard Roach, S.J., "Sex in Christian Morality," *Way,* 11 (1971), pp. 148-61; 235-42.
27. Gabriel Marcel, *Creative Fidelity,* translated by Robert Rosthal. (New York: Farrar, Straus, 1964 ed.), p. 153. Cf. Albert Dondeyne, *Contemporary European Thought and Christian Faith.* Translated by Ernan McMullin and John Burnheim. (Pittsburgh: Duquesne University Press, 1958), p. 63.
28. See Guzman Carriquiry, "Sexuality and Asceticism," in *Commentaries on the Vatican Declaration on Sexual Ethics,* p. 84.
29. Carriquiry, p. 84.
30. Carriquiry, pp. 76-78.
31. See Fuchs, *Human Values,* pp. 100-101; 120-131.

CHAPTER 4

1. See Kosnik *et al., Human Sexuality,* p. 11.
2. See Paul K. Jewett, *Man as Male and Female* (Grand Rapids, MI: Wm. B. Eerdmans, 1975), p. 20.
3. See Kosnik, *et al., Human Sexuality,* p. 13.

4. Jewett, *Man as Male and Female,* p. 95.
5. See John L. McKenzie, S.J., "Woman," in *Dictionary of the Bible* (Milwaukee: Bruce, 1965 ed.), p. 936.
6. See Leonard Swidler, "Jesus Was a Feminist," *Catholic World* 212 (1971), pp. 177-183. Cf. Jewett, *Man as Male and Female,* pp. 94-103. See especially C.F.D. Moule, *The Phenomenon of the New Testament* (Naperville, IL: Allenson, 1967), pp. 151-156.
7. See Kosnik *et al., Human Sexuality,* p. 20.
8. See M. Strack and P. Billerbeck, *Kommentar zum Neuen Testament aus Talmud und Midrasch* (Munich: C.H. Beck, 1926), pp. 312-314.
9. Strack and Billerbeck, p. 320.
10. See Strack and Billerbeck, p. 320.
11. Kosnik *et al., Human Sexuality,* p. 28. See Jewett, *Man as Male and Female,* p. 86.
12. Kosnik, *et al.,* p. 28.
13. See Rosemary Ruether, "Is Christianity Misogynist?" in *Liberation Theology: Human Hope Confronts Christian History and American Power,* edited by Rosemary Ruether (New York: Paulist Press, 1971), pp. 95-114.
14. Tertullian, *On the Appeal of Women, Book 1* in *The Ante-Nicene Fathers, Vol. 4* (New York: Charles Scribner's Sons, 1926), p. 14.
15. Saint Jerome, *Letter 54* in *A Select Library of Nicene and Post-Nicene Fathers of the Christian Church, Vol. 6* (Grand Rapids, MI: Eerdmans, 1928), pp. 104-107.
16. Saint Augustine, *Soliloquies, Book I, Chapter 10* in *The Fathers of the Church: A New Translation* (New York: Cima, 1948), pp. 365-66.
17. Saint Thomas Aquinas, *Summa Theologica, I-I,* ques. 1, art. 1.
18. On this 40/80 day theory see Russell Shaw, *Abortion on Trial* (Dayton, OH: Pflaum Press, 1968), pp. 169-171.
19. For some interesting background in this area see Letty M. Russell, *Human Liberation in a Feminist Perspective: A Theology.* (Philadelphia: Fortress Press, 1973).
20. Noted in Helmut Thielicke, *The Ethics of Sex* (Grand Rapids, MI: Baker Book House, 1964), p. 146.
21. For a good summary of the problem of pedastalism see Mary Daly, *The Church and the Second Sex* (New York: Harper & Row, 1975), pp. 147-165.
22. See Keane, *Sexual Morality,* p. 23.
23. For an excellent history of women in America see Eleanor Flexner, *Century of Struggle: The Women's Rights Movement in the United States* (Cambridge: Belknap Press, 1959).
24. See Keane, *Sexual Morality,* p. 24.
25. Keane, pp. 25-26.
26. For an interesting overview see A.M. Gardiner, ed., *Women and the Catholic Priesthood* (New York: Paulist Press, 1976).
27. See Keane, *Sexual Morality,* p. 29.
28. See Keane, p. 30.

29. See Keane, p. 30.
30. Although a great deal of caution is needed here lest the physical argument be pushed too far and extended into areas where it should not apply, it is sometimes valid. Persons hired to model women's clothes will be women. Most women (but not all) may lack the physical strength needed for some jobs. Some men, of course, will also lack that strength.
31. Since all human life is relational, the difference in relational consciousness may be said to enter into all its aspects (without this fact excluding anyone from jobs, etc.). Thus our statement of relationality is the focal point for interpreting the differences between the sexes as a beginning rather than an ending of our reflection. The difference in relational consciousness not only stresses the importance of our responsibilities to the opposite sex; it also enriches the quality of our relationships to members of our own sex. For an excellent theological analysis see Margaret Farley, R.S.M., "New Patterns of Relationship: Beginnings of a Moral Revolution," in *Woman: New Dimensions,* edited by Walter Burghardt, S.J. (New York: Paulist Press, 1977), pp. 51-70.

CHAPTER 5

1. See Bernard Lonergan, S.J., *Method in Theology* (London: Darton, Longman & Todd, 1970), pp. 319-320.
2. See Henry deLaszlo and Paul Henshaw, "Plant Materials Used by Primitive Peoples to Affect Fertility," *Science,* 119 (1954), p. 626.
3. See Philip Wheelwright, ed., *Aristotle* (New York: The Odyssey Press, 1951), pp. 112-113.
4. Hippocrates, "Oath" in *Medical Works, Vol. I* edited and translated by W.M.H. Jones (Cambridge, MA: Loeb Classical Library, 1957), p. 298.
5. See Saint Ambrose, "Hexaemeron" in *Patrologia Latina* 5:18, 58: "The poor abandon their children; rich women deny their own fetus in their uterus and by harmful potions extinguish the pledges of their womb in their genital belly. Cf. Adolphe Landry, "La depopulation dans l'antiquite," *Revue historique* 177 (1936), pp. 1-5. Also, Jerome Carcopino, *Daily Life in Ancient Rome,* translated by E.O. Lorimer (New Haven, CT: Yale University Press, 1940), p. 90.
6. See John T. Noonan, *Contraception* (Cambridge, MA: Harvard University Press, 1965), pp. 30-36.
7. See Noonan, p. 35.
8. See A.M. DuBarle, "La Bible et les Peres ont-ils parle de la contraception?," *La Vie Spirituelle* 15 (1962 Supplement), pp. 575-576.
9. See Noonan, *Contraception,* pp. 37-38.
10. See Noonan, p. 39.
11. See James Gustafson, *Protestant and Roman Catholic Ethics* (Chicago, IL: University of Chicago Press, 1978), pp. 50-51.
12. See Noonan, *Contraception,* pp. 44-45.
13. See Noonan, p. 48.
14. See Noonan, pp. 46-47.

15. See Noonan, p. 58.
16. See Charles Curran, "Absolute Norms in Moral Theology," *A New Look at Christian Morality* (Notre Dame, IN: Fides, 1965), pp. 75-79.
17. Saint John Chrysostom, "Homily on the Epistle to Titus," in *Patrologia Graeca,* 62:689.
18. Saint Ambrose, "Exposition on the Gospel according to Luke 1:43-45," in *The Post-Nicene Fathers,* 32:38-39.
19. Saint Jerome, "On Galatians," in *Patrologia Latina,* 26:443.
20. Jean-Paul Audet, *La Didache: Instructions des Apotres* (Paris, 1958), p. 197.
21. See Noonan, *Contraception,* pp. 119-126.
22. Saint Augustine, *On the Good of Marriage,* chap. 7, par. 6.
23. See Noonan, *Contraception,* p. 133.
24. See Noonan, p. 135.
25. See Noonan, p. 143.
26. Saint Gregory the Great, "Pastoral Rule," *Patrologia Latina* 3:27, 77:102.
27. Regino of Prum, "Churchly Disciplines and the Christian Religion," *Patrologia Latina,* 132:301.
28. See Noonan, *Contraception,* p. 178.
29. See Noonan, p. 182-83.
30. See Noonan, p. 222.
31. See Noonan, p. 224.
32. See Noonan, p. 238.
33. Saint Thomas Aquinas, *Summa Theologica, II-II* ques. 154 art, 12, obj. 1.
34. This is the interpretation that can be found in this early work of Josef Fuchs, S.J., *Die Sexualethik des heiliger. Thomas von Aquin* (Cologne, 1949), p. 181.
35. See Noonan, *Contraception,* pp. 276-279.
36. See Noonan, p. 279.
37. See Noonan, pp. 282-283. This axiom was and still is quite popular in Thomistic circles. See, for example, Avery Dulles, S.J., *Introductory Metaphysics* (New York: Sheed & Ward, 1955), pp. 90-91.
38. See Noonan, p. 295.
39. See Noonan, p. 306, note 2.
40. See the classical study by Louis Vereecke, C.Ss.R., "Marriage et sexualite au declin du moyen age," *La Vie Spirituelle,* 14 (1961 Supplement), pp. 199, 200; 220-224.
41. Vereecke, p. 224.
42. See Noonan, *Contraception,* p. 324.
43. See Noonan, pp. 330; 327.
44. See Noonan, pp. 346-347.
45. The decree of Sixtus can be found in *Sedes Apostolica: Magnum bullarium romanum* (Luxembourg, 1942), p. 766. See Noonan, *Contraception,* p. 363.
46. See Noonan, *Contraception,* p. 363. See Ludwig Pastor, *History of the Popes* (St. Louis: B. Herder & Co., 1953), p. 90.
47. Saint Alphonsus Liguori, *Istruzione practica per i confessori* (Torino, 1895).

48. See Noonan, *Contraception,* p. 365.
49. See Kingsley Davis, *The Theory of Change and Response in Demographic History* (Berkeley: University of California Press, 1963), p. 350.
50. See Davis, p. 350.
51. *Decisiones Sanctae Sedis* (Roma: Vatican Polyglot Press), pp. 11-12.
52. "De usu onanastico matrimonii," in *D.S.2715,* p. 546.
53. "De usu," D.S. *2795,* p. 560.
54. Liguori, *Istruzione practica....*p. 375.
55. See Paul MeKeever, "Seventy-Five Years of Moral Theology in America," *American Ecclesiastical Review,* 152 (1965), pp. 17-19.
56. See Noonan, *Contraception,* pp. 406-408.
57. *The Lambeth Conference,* par. 15.
58. Pope Leo XIII, *Arcanum Divinae Sapientiae, Il Matrimonio* (Roma: Edizioni Paoline, 1973 ed.), pp. 115-149.
59. Vermeersch set this forth in his academic treatise *De castitate et de vitiis contrariis* (Roma: Pontifica Universitas Gregoriana, 1919), p. 270. This supported the thought of Jerome Noldin, *De sexto praecepto et de usu matrimonii.* (Innsbruck, Austria, 1911), p. 86. See also, Vermeersch, "Un grave peril moral," *Nouvelle Revue Theologique* 41 (1909), pp. 65-72. Also, Vermeersch, "La Conference de Lambeth et la morale du marriage," in *Nouvelle Revue Theologique* 57 (1930), pp. 850-860.
60. Pope Pius XI, *Casti Connubii,* par. 316 in *Il Matrimonio,* p. 227.
61. Pius XI, par. 326, p. 233.
62. Pius XI, par. 317, p. 228.
63. Pius XI, par. 317, p. 228.
64. See Charles Singer and E. Ashworth Underwood, *A Short History of Medicine* (Oxford: Oxford University Press, 1928), p. 204.
65. Kyusaku Ogino, *Conception Period of Women,* translated by Yonez Miyagawa (Harrisburg, PA: 1934) and Hermann Knaus, *Periodic Fertility and Sterilization in Women,* translated by D.H. and Kathleen Kitchin (Vienna, 1934).
66. Pope Pius XII, "Allocuzione alle ostetriche," in *Il Matrimonio,* par. 622, p. 390.
67. Hyacinth Hering, O.P., "De *amplexu reservato,"Angelicum* 28 (1951), p. 333; 338-340.
68. *Decisiones Sanctae Sedis,* pp. 40-41.
69. Francis Hurth, S.J., "Inquisitio critica in moralitatem *amplexus reservati,"* Periodica 41 (1952), p. 265.
70. John Ford and Gerald Kelly, *Contemporary Moral Theology, Vol. II* (Westminster, MD: Newman Press, 1961 ed.), pp. 222-223.
71. Francis Connell, "The Use of Anaphrodisiacs," *American Ecclesiastical Review,* 136 (1957), p. 55.
72. Pope Pius XII, "Allocuzione alle ostetriche," par. 614, p. 387.
73. See J. Ghoos, "L'acte a *double effet:* Etude de theologie positive," *Ephemerides theologicae lovaniensis,* 27 (1951). Cf. Joseph Mangan, "An Historical Analysis of the Principle of Double Effect," *Theological Studies* 10 (1949); Gerald Kelly, "Pius XII and the Principle of Totality," *Theological Studies,* 16 (1955), p. 373; Bert Cunningham, *The Morality of*

Organic Transplantation (Washington, D.C.), pp. 100-104; T.V. Moore, "The Morality of Sterilizing Operations," *American Ecclesiastical Review,* 106 (1942), pp. 444-446. Also to be noted is the fact that during the years 1946-1953 much was printed in *Theological Studies* in the section entitled "Notes on Moral Theology," edited by Ford and Kelly.

74. See John Lynch, "Fertility Control and the Moral Law," *Linacre Quarterly,* 20 (1953), pp. 83-89.
75. See John Rock, *The Time Has Come* (New York: Alfred Knopf), pp. 142-156.
76. See Francis Connell, "The Contraceptive Pill," *American Ecclesiastical Review,* 137 (1957). Cf. Louis Janssens, "Morale conjugale et progesterones," *Ephemerides Theologicae Louvaniensis,* 39 (1963), p. 790.
77. See the statement made in the Boston Archdiocese newspaper *The Pilot,* May 9, 1963.
78. See Louis Janssens, "Morale conjugale et progesterones," p. 790.
79. *Acta Apostolicae Sedis,* 56:588.

CHAPTER 6

1. A concise and yet very informative collection and distillation of the reactions to the papal encyclical can be found in Leo Pyle, ed., *Pope and Pill* (London: Darton, Longman & Todd, 1968). Perhaps the most comprehensive multilingual bibliography compiled to date on *Humanae Vitae* can be found in Giuseppe Besutti O.S.M., "Contribuito Bibliografico sulla *Humanae Vitae," Lateranum,* n. 1 (1978), pp. 276-364.
2. Dogmatic Constitution, *Pastor Aeternus, D.S.* 3074, p. 601.
3. See John Coulson, "Living with Authority: The Nineteenth Century" in *Contraception: Authority and Dissent,* edited by Charles Curran (New York: Herder & Herder, 1969), pp. 19-40.
4. Joseph Komonchak, "Ordinary Papal Magisterium and Religious Assent" in *Contraception: Authority and Dissent,* pp. 101-126. Cf. *Lumen Gentium,* par. 25 and *Gaudium et Spes,* par. 62.
5. See Dionigi Tettamanzi, "Il Magistero delle Conferenze Episcopali Europee e la *Humanae Vitae," Lateranum,* pp. 48-91. See also John Cardinal Wright, "Reaction of Anglophone Hierarchies to *Humanae Vitae," Lateranum,* pp. 92-104.
6. See Komonchak, pp. 121-126. Cf. Daniel Maguire, "Moral Inquiry and Religious Assent," in *Contraception: Authority and Dissent,* pp. 127-148.
7. See Pyle, pp. 75-85.
8. Pyle, "The Birth Control Report: The Conservative Case," *Pope and Pill,* pp. 280-81.
9. Pyle, p. 272.
10. Pyle, p. 273.
11. Pyle, p. 281.
12. See Bernard Haring, C.Ss.R., "The Inseparability of the Unitive and Procreative Functions of the Marital Act," in *Contraception: Authority and Dissent,* p. 180.

13. See McHugh and Callan, *Moral Theology, Vol. I,* pp. 22-23.
14. Pyle, p. 285.
15. See Josef Fuchs, S.J., *Natural Law,* translated by Helmut Reckter (New York: Sheed & Ward, 1965), pp. 154-156.
16. See Karol Wojtyla, "La visione anthropologica della *Humanae Vitae,*" *Lateranum,* pp. 127-133.
17. Saint Thomas Aquinas, *Summa Theologica,* I-II, ques. 94; II-II ques. 106, articles 1 and 2.
18. See Haring, *Free and Faithful, Vol. I,* p. 231.
19. See Haring, pp. 324-327.
20. Pyle, pp. 284-285.
21. Pyle (ed.), "The Birth Control Report: The Majority View," *Pope and Pill,* p. 267.
22. Pyle, p. 270.
23. See Haring in *Contraception: Authority and Dissent,* p. 190.
24. Pyle, p. 263.
25. *Humanae Vitae,* par. 12.
26. *Humanae Vitae,* par. 16: "The Church teaches that it is then licit to take into account the natural rhythms immanent in the generative functions, for the use of marriage in the infecund periods only, and in this way to regulate birth without offending the moral principles which have been recalled earlier."
27. *Humanae Vitae,* par. 13.
28. *Humanae Vitae,* par. 14: "We must again declare that the direct intervention of the generative process already begun, and above all, directly willed and procured abortion, even if for therapeutic reasons, are to be absolutely excluded as licit means of regulating birth...."
29. *Humanae Vitae,* par. 15.
30. *Humanae Vitae,* par. 11.
31. *Humanae Vitae,* par. 13; 16.
32. *Humanae Vitae,* par. 13.
33. See Haring in *Contraception: Authority and Dissent,* p. 180.
34. *Humanae Vitae,* par. 16.
35. See Guindon, *Sexual Language,* pp. 204-220.
36. *Humanae Vitae,* par. 18.
37. See Sidney Callahan, *Beyond Birth Control: The Christian Experience of Sex* (New York: Sheed & Ward, 1968), pp. 141-144.
38. See Barnabas Ahern, C.P., "Christian Holiness and Chastity," in *Commentaries on the Vatican Declaration on Sexual Ethics,* pp. 115-116.
39. See Guindon, *Sexual Language,* pp. 89-90.
40. Fuchs, *Human Values and Christian Morality,* p. 101.

CHAPTER 7

1. See Clive Wood, *Human Fertility: Threat and Promise* (New York: Funk & Wagnalls, 1968), pp. 8-31.
2. See Ann Kramer, ed., *Woman's Body* (London: Paddington Press, 1977), p. A-13.

3. See Wood, *Human Fertility,* pp. 68-69.
4. See Gerhard Doring, "Detection of Ovulation by the Basal Body Temperature Method," Urricchio, ed., *Proceedings of a Research Conference on Natural Family Planning,* pp. 172-173.
5. See Callahan, *Beyond Birth Control,* pp. 192-193; *Humanae Vitae,* par. 25.
6. Callahan, pp. 195-203.
7. See Thomas O'Donnell, S.J., *Medicine and Christian Morality* (New York: Alba House, 1976 ed.), pp. 192-194.
8. From a theological point of view, this possibility was first presented by Bernard Haring C.Ss.R., "New Dimensions of Responsible Parenthood," *Theological Studies,* 37 (1976), pp. 120-132. Cf. Thomas Hilgers, "Human Reproduction: Three Issues for the Moral Theologian," *Theological Studies* (March 1977), pp. 136-152. From the medical and scientific point of view, we note Rodrigo Guerrero, "Possible Effects of the Periodic Abstinence Method," in *Proceedings...,* pp. 96-110. Marie-Claire Orgebin-Crist, "Sperm Age: Effects on Zygote Development," in *Proceedings...,* pp. 85-95.
9. See John Billings, *Natural Family Planning: The Ovulation Method* (Collegeville, MN: Liturgical Press, 1973), p. 13.
10. Billings, p. 12.
11. Billings, p. 13.
12. Billings, p. 13.
13. See John Marshall, "Prediction, Detection, and Control of Ovulation: An Overview," in *Proceedings...,* pp. 135-148.
14. For a good introduction in this regard see Anthony Zimmerman, S.V.D. ed., *A Reader in Natural Family Planning* (Collegeville, IN: Human Life Center, 1978).
15. John Peel and Malcolm Potts eds., *Textbook of Contraceptive Practice* (Cambridge: Cambridge University Press, 1970), pp. 49-51.
16. See Peel and Potts, p. 51.
17. Peel and Potts, p. 52.
18. Peel and Potts, p. 71.
19. Peel and Potts, pp. 74-79.
20. Peel and Potts, pp. 130-131.
21. Peel and Potts, p. 134.
22. Peel and Potts, p. 136.
23. Peel and Potts, pp. 90-98.
24. Peel and Potts, p. 106.
25. Wood, *Human Fertility,* p. 137.
26. Wood, p. 138.
27. Peel and Potts, *Textbook of Contraceptive Practice,* p. 259.
28. Peel and Potts, p. 260.

CHAPTER 8

1. See *Gaudium et Spes,* par. 48: "By their very nature, the institution of matrimony itself and conjugal love are ordained for the procreation and education of children, and find in them their ultimate crown."

2. *Gaudium et Spes,* par. 48.
3. See *Gaudium et Spes,* par. 50: "They will thoughtfully take into account both their own welfare and that of their children, those already born and those which may be foreseen. For this accounting they will reckon with both the material and the spiritual conditions of the times as well as of their state in life."
4. *Gaudium et Spes,* par. 50.
5. See *Gaudium et Spes,* par. 51.
6. *Gaudium et Spes,* par. 50.
7. See *Gaudium et Spes,* par. 51.
8. See *Gaudium et Spes,* par. 51.
9. *Gaudium et Spes,* par. 50.
10. See our previous reflections on this point in Chapter 3.
11. See Haring, *Free and Faithful, Vol. I.*
12. See Andre Hellegers, "A Scientist's Analysis," in *Contraception: Authority and Dissent,* pp. 216-236; 237-239.
13. See Pedro Beltrao, "La Populazione mondiale as una svolta storica," *Lateranum,* pp. 256-275.
14. See Callahan, *Beyond Birth Control,* pp. 207-247.
15. *Humanae Vitae,* par. 17.

CHAPTER 9

1. See Kramer, ed., *Woman's Body,* p. C-13; Cf. Kosnik, *et al., Human Sexuality,* p. 128.
2. Pope Pius XI, *Casti Connubii,* par. 327-28 in *Il Matrimonio,* pp. 233-34.
3. *Acta Apostolica Sedis* 23 (1931), 119.
4. Pope Pius XI, "Allocuzione al Sacro Collegio," in *Il Matrimonio,* n. 406-07, p. 270.
5. *Acta Apostolica Sedis* 32 (1940), 73.
6. "De sterilizatione," DS 3788, p. 741.
7. Pope Pius XII, "Allocuzione alle ostetriche," in *Il Matrimonio,* p. 387.
8. Pope Pius XII, "Allocuzione al XXVI Congresso d'urologia," n. 693 in *Il Matrimonio,* p. 423.
9. Pyle, ed., *Pope and Pill,* p. 267.
10. *Humanae Vitae,* par. 14.
11. U.S.C.C., *The Code of Ethical and Religious Directives for Catholic Health-Care Facilities* (Washington, D.C.: U.S.C.C., 1971), n. 2, p. 6.
12. N.C.C.B., *Letter of Most Rev. Joseph Bernadin.* (Washington, D.C.: N.C.C.B., April 11, 1975).
13. For an outline of the cases of sterilization that have been accepted under the traditional understanding of the principle of double effects see Thomas O'Donnell, S.J., *Medicine and Christian Morality* (New York: Alba House, 1975 ed.), pp. 114-118.
14. Pope Pius XII, "Allocuzione alle ostetriche," p. 387.
15. See Keane, *Sexual Morality,* p. 130.
16. See Keane, p. 130.

17. See Leslie Westoff, "Vas Deferens in Vasectomies," *Esquire* (March 1, 1978), pp. 25-26.
18. See O'Donnell, *Medicine and Christian Morality,* p. 116.
19. *Humanae Vitae,* par. 14.
20. See Keane, *Sexual Morality,* pp. 130-131, Cf. Richard McCormick, S.J., "Medico-Moral Opinions: Vasectomy and Sterilization," *The Linacre Quarterly* 38 (1971), pp. 9-10.
21. See Lawrence Wrenn, *Annulments* (Hartford, CT: Canon Law Society, 1970), pp. 78-84.
22. See John Dedek, *Contemporary Medical Ethics* (Kansas City: Sheed, Andrews, and McMeel Inc., 1976), p. 76.
23. N.C.C.B., *The Code of Directives.*
24. "Reply of the Sacred Congregation of the Faith," (March 13, 1975) Prot. 2027/69.
25. Richard McCormick, S.J., "Sterilization and Theological Method," *Theological Studies* 37 (Sept. 1976), pp. 471-77.
26. McCormick, pp. 471-77.
27. See Keane, *Sexual Morality,* pp. 130-131.
28. See McCormick, "Sterilization and Theological Method," pp. 471-77.

CHAPTER 10

1. See David Heidenstam, *Man's Body* (London: Paddington Press, 1976), p. K-32.
2. Alfred Kinsey, *Sexual Behavior in the Human Male* (Philadelphia: Saunders, 1948), p. 499-510.
3. Shere Hite, *The Hite Report* (New York: Macmillan, 1976), pp. 3-58.
4. Kinsey, *Sexual Behavior in the Human Male,* pp. 499-510; *Sexual Behavior in the Human Female* (Philadelphia: Saunders, 1953), p. 520.
5. Albert Ellis, *Sex Without Guilt* (New York: L. Stuart 1958). Cf. W.B. Pomeroy, *Sex and Boys* (New York: Delacorte Press, 1968), p. 38.
6. Masters and Johnson, *Human Sexual Inadequacy,* pp. 95-6.
7. See E.B. Hurlock, *Adolescent Development* (New York: McGraw Hill, 1966).
8. See T.C. deKruijf, *The Bible on Sexuality* (De Pere, WI: St. Norbert Abbey Press, 1966), p.40.
9. For a classic example of this see Noldin, *De sexto praecepto et de usu matrimonii,* p. 76. For a newer look see Charles Curran, "Masturbation and Objectively Grave Matter," *A New Look at Christian Morality,* pp. 200-221.
10. See Curran, p. 30.
11. See Kosnik, *et al., Human Sexuality,* p. 220.
12. See Fuchs, *De castitate et de ordine sexuali,* p. 68.
13. Kosnik, *et al., Human Sexuality,* p. 220.
14. Kosnik, *et al.,* p. 220.
15. DS. 687, 688.
16. "Errares doctrinae moralis laxioris" in DS. 2149.

17. Zalba cites this in *Theologia moralis summa, Vol. II,* p. 160.
18. *"De masturbatione directe procurata,"* D.S. 3684.
19. *Acta Apostolicae Sedis* 44 (1952) 275.
20. *Religiosorum institutio,* n. 30.
21. N.C.C.B., *Ethical and Religious Directives,* n. 21, p. 7.
22. *A Guide to Formation in Priestly Celibacy,* n. 63, p. 54.
23. *Persona Humana,* par. 9.
24. *Education in Human Sexuality,* p. 34.
25. Cf. Russell Abata, *Sex, Sanity in the Modern World.* (St. Louis: Liguorian Books, 1975), p. 48.
26. See William Bausch, *A Boy's Sex Life: Handbook of Basic Information and Guidance* (Notre Dame, IN: Fides, 1969).
27. See O'Neil and Donovan, *Sexuality and Moral Responsibility,* p. 107.
28. See O'Neil and Donovan, pp. 108-109.
29. See O'Neil and Donovan, p. 109.
30. See O'Neil and Donovan, p. 109.
31. See O'Neil and Donovan, p. 105.

CHAPTER 11

1. O'Donnell, *Medicine and Christian Morality,* p. 263.
2. Bernard Haring, C.Ss.R., *Ethics of Manipulation* (New York: Seabury, 1975), p. 194.
3. Haring, p. 194.
4. Pope Pius XII, "Allocuzione al Congresso internazionale dei medici cattolici," *Il Matrimonio,* pp. 256-57.
5. Pope Pius XII, "Allocuzione alle ostetriche," p. 397. "The conjugal act, ordained and willed by nature, is a personal act of cooperation, the right to which husband and wife give to each other when they marry..."
6. Haring, *Ethics of Manipulation,* p. 195.
7. Before the papal statement of 1949, a number of balanced and even rather conservative moralists such as Gerald Kelly and Arthur Vermeersch approved of AIH, at least when the sperm was obtained in a licit way. See, for example, Gerald Kelly, "The Morality of Artificial Insemination," *American Ecclesiastical Review* (1939), p. 113.
8. For the trend of theological debate before and after the Pope's intervention see *Theological Studies* 8 (1947), pp. 106-110; n. 10 (1949), pp. 113-114; n. 11 (1950), pp. 67-69.
9. See James Nelson, *Human Medicine: Ethical Perspectives on New Medical Issues* (MN: Augsburg, 1973), p. 70.
10. Paul Ramsey, *Fabricated Man* (New Haven: Yale University Press, 1970), p. 131.
11. Joseph Fletcher, *Morals and Medicine* (Boston: Beacon Press, 1954), p. 139.
12. George Lobo, S.J., *Current Problems in Medical Ethics* (Westminster, MD: Christian Classics, 1974), p. 132.
13. Haring, *Medical Ethics,* p. 92.

14. Kosnik *et al., Human Sexuality,* p. 138-39.
15. Nelson, *Human Medicine,* p. 72.
16. Quoted in John Gordon, "Artificial Insemination: Some Legal Considerations," in *Soundings,* Vol. liv, n. 3 (Fall 1971), p. 313.
17. Nelson, *Human Medicine,* p. 73.
18. Nelson, p. 77.
19. Nelson, p. 77.
20. Nelson, p. 78.
21. Haring, *Ethics of Manipulation,* p. 197.
22. Ramsey, *Fabricated Man,* p. 128.
23. Karl Rahner, S.J., "Zum Problem der genetischen Manipulation," *Schrften zue Theologie* (Benziger: Zurich), pp. 313-315.

CHAPTER 12

1. See Gerald Kelly, S.J., *Modern Youth and Chastity.* (St. Louis: Liguorian, 1946), pp. 74-76.
2. Obviously it is detrimental to speak of persons as occasions of sin. Nevertheless, this approach and the approach of most of the manuals of the 1950s speak in this way.
3. See Kosnik *et al., Human Sexuality,* p. 177.
4. See Kosnik, *et al.,* p. 179.
5. See Kosnik, *et al.,* p. 179.
6. See Keane, *Sexual Morality,* pp. 161-62.
7. See Nelson, *Embodiment,* pp. 227-28.
8. See James McCarry, *Sexual Myths and Fantasies* (New York: Schocken Books, 1971), p. 39.
9. See *Gaudium et Spes,* par. 12.
10. See Nelson, *Embodiment,* pp. 16-18.
11. See Keane, *Sexual Morality,* p. 152.
12. See Keane, p. 152.
13. See Keane, p. 153.
14. See Kennedy, *The New Sexuality,* pp. 33-45.
15. Bruno Maggioni, "Rapporti pre-matrimoniali: reflessioni bibliche," *Rapporti Pre-matrimoniali e Coscienza Christiana,* edited by Pino Sabini and Giorgio Campanini (Roma: Editrice A.V.E., 1979), pp. 237-257.
16. Dionigi Tettamanzi, "I rapporti pre-matrimoniali nella tradizione cristiana," *Rapporti Pre-matrimoniale,* pp. 259-309.
17. "Fornicatio est copula soluti cum soluta ex mutuo consensu" in Noldin, *De Sexto Praecepto,* Vol. I, 3; 1/2.
18. According to Saint Thomas, the sins against chastity, but not against nature, are fornication, adultery, rape, incest, seduction, and sacrilege, that is, intercourse involving irreligion. Sins against both chastity and nature are masturbation, birth control, homosexual activity, and bestiality. See *Summa Theologica* II-II, ques. 154.
19. Saint Alphonsus Liguori, *Theologia Moralis,* Vol. III, p. 432.
20. Vermeersch, *De Castitate,* par. 304.

21. Fuchs, *De Castitate et Ordine Sexuali,* p. 100.
22. Maggioni, *Rapporti Pre-matrimoniali, pp. 246-253.*
23. *Saint Alphonsus Liguori, Theologia Moralis,* Vol. III, p. 432.
24. Vermeersch, *De Castitate,* par. 304.
25. See Kosnik *et al., Human Sexuality,* p. 156. However, the problem of venereal disease has emerged again so as to be relevant to the moral question. The incidence of gonorrhea and syphillis has grown by leaps and bounds. See Guindon, *Sexual Language,* pp. 395-404.
26. See Kosnik, *et al.,* p. 157.
27. See *Persona Humana,* par. 7.
28. See *Persona Humana,* par. 7.
29. For an example of this rigid viewpoint see Henry Davis, *Moral and Pastoral Theology* (London: Sheed & Ward, 1936), pp. 177-178, 180-182.
30. For an interesting evaluation see Richard McCormick, "Notes on Moral Theology," *Theological Studies,* 34 (March 1973), p. 77-92.
31. See Kosnik *et al., Human Sexuality,* p. 161.
32. For an accurate presentation of this approach see the following statement presented to the United Presbyterian Church of America, *The Study Document on Sexuality and the Human Community:* "Responsibly appropriate behavior might be defined as sexual expression which is proportional to the depth and maturity of the relationship and to the degree to which it approaches the permanence of the marriage covenant...."
33. See Kosnik *et al., Human Sexuality,* p. 163. See also, Lester Kirkendall, "A New Bill of Sexual Rights and Responsibilities," *The Humanist,* 36 (Jan.-Feb. 1976), p. 5.
34. Kinsey, *Sexual Behavior in the Human Female,* p. 292.
35. Kinsey, p. 292.
36. See Vance Packard, *The Sexual Wilderness* (Ontario: Pocket Books, 1970).
37. Gallup Poll, Detroit Free Press, October 5, 1975.
38. Shirley Saldahna, "American Catholics: Ten Years Later," *The Critic,* 33 (1975), p. 18.
39. Andrew Greeley, *The Catholic Priest in the United States: A Sociological Investigation* (Washington, D.C.: U.S.C.C., 1972), p. 101.

CHAPTER 13

1. Snow, "Changing Patterns of Marriage," in *Male and Female,* p. 63.
2. Snow, p. 64.
3. See David Ludwig, "That Troubled Institution Called Marriage," in *Currents in Theology and Mission,* vol. 5. n. 3 (June 1978), p. 159.
4. Ludwig, p. 160. For the effects of the mass-media on sexuality see also Albert Ellis, *The American Sexual Tragedy* (New York: Grove Press, 1962), pp. 16-17.
5. See Robert T. Francoeur, "The Technologies of Man-Made Sex," in *The Future of Sexual Relations,* edited by Robert and Anna Francoeur (Englewood Cliffs, NJ: Prentice-Hall, 1974), pp. 3-11.

6. See Jessie Barnard, *The Sex Game* (Englewood Cliffs, NJ: Prentice-Hall, 1971), p. 38.
7. See the study of Gerhard Neubeck (ed.), *Extra-Marital Relations* (Englewood Cliffs, NJ: Prentice-Hall, 1969).
8. Donald Conroy, "The Statistics and Crisis of Divorce," *The Living Light,* vol. 13, n. 4 (Winter 1976), p. 548.
9. Jessie Barnard, "No News, but New Ideas," in *Divorce and After,* pp. 1-29.
10. Brian Boylan, *Infidelity* (Englewood Cliffs, NJ: Prentice-Hall, 1971), p. 2.
11. The empirical data would be a study in and of itself.
12. Morton Hunt, *The Affair: A Portrait of Extra-Marital Love in Contemporary America* (New York: New American Library, 1969).
13. See Anthony Pietropinto, M.D. and Jacqueline Simenauer, *Beyond the Male Myth: A Nationwide Survey* (New York: New York Times Book Co., 1977), pp. 282-283.
14. Robert T. Francoeur, *Eve's New Rib: Twenty Faces of Sex, Marriage, and Family* (New York: Harcourt, Brace, Jovanovich, 1972), p. 109.
15. Francoeur, p. 110.
16. Raymond Lawrence, "Toward a More Flexible Monogamy," in *The Future of Sexual Relations,* p. 68.
17. Lawrence, p. 68.
18. See Kosnik *et al., Human Sexuality,* pp. 145-146.

CHAPTER 14

1. See Katchadourian and Lunde, *Fundamentals of Human Sexuality,* pp. 265-266.
2. See Katchadourian and Lunde, p. 266.
3. See Katchadourian and Lunde, p. 269.
4. See Katchadourian and Lunde, p. 268. Cf. Guindon, *The Sexual Language,* p. 302.
5. C.S. Ford and F.A. Beach, *Patterns of Sexual Behavior* (New York: Harper & Row, 1951), pp. 134-143.
6. Norman Pittenger, *A Time for Consent* (London: SCM Press, 1970), pp. 27-41.
7. See Guindon, *Sexual Language,* pp. 342-343.
8. See Keane, *Sexual Morality,* pp. 74-75.
9. See Katchadourian and Lunde, *Fundamantals of Human Sexuality,* p. 267.
10. See Katchadourian and Lunde, p. 270.
11. See Katchadourian and Lunde, p. 271.
12. See Guindon, *Sexual Language,* p. 306.
13. To date, no single theory seems adequate.
14. See Guindon, *Sexual Language,* pp. 307-309.
15. See Paul Ecker, "Homosexuality: Genetic and Dynamic Factor," in *Personality and Sexual Problems,* edited by William Bier, S.J. (New York: Fordham University Press, 1964), pp. 160-161.
16. See Keane, *Sexual Morality,* pp. 83-84.

17. See the pamphlet *Homosexual Catholics: A Primer for Discussion.*
18. See Kennedy, *The New Sexuality,* p. 130.
19. See Martin Noth, *Leviticus: A Commentary* (London: SCM Press, 1965), p. 16.
20. See Kosnik *et al., Human Sexuality,* p. 189.
21. See Kosnik, *et al.,* p. 190.
22. See Gerhard vonRad, *Genesis: A Commentary* (Philadelphia: Westminster Press, 1961), pp. 212-213. The Jesuit author John P. McNeil leans heavily upon this interpretation. See *The Church and the Homosexual* (New York: Pocket Books, 1976), pp. 53-61.
23. See Kosnik *et al., Human Sexuality,* p. 190.
24. See Kosnik *et al.,* p. 192.
25. See McNeil, *The Church and the Homosexual,* p. 63.
26. See McNeil, pp. 65-67.
27. See McNeil, p. 69.
28. Saint Augustine, *Confessions,* 3, 8; Saint John Chrystostom, in *Epistulam ad Romanum* in *Patrologia Graeca,* IV, 60.
29. D.S. Bailey, *Homosexuality and the Western Christian Tradition* (London: Longmans, Green, 1955), p. 157.
30. See Kosnik *et al., Human Sexuality,* p. 197.
31. See Kosnik, *et al.,* p. 197.
32. Saint Thomas Aquinas, *Summa Theologica,* II-II, ques. 154, art. 11-12.
33. See Guindon, *The Sexual Language,* p. 338. Cf. Bailey, *Homosexuality and the Western Christian Tradition,* p. 164.
34. N.C.C.B., "Principles to Guide Confessors in Questions of Homosexuality," (Washington, D.C.: N.C.C.B., 1973), p. 3.
35. *Persona Humana,* par. 8.
36. N.C.C.B., *To Live in Christ Jesus* (Washington, D.C.: U.S.C.C., 1976), p. 19. For a good pastoral approach see the pastoral letter of Bishop Francis Mugavero of Brooklyn, "The Gift of Sexuality," printed in *Origins* 5 (1976), pp. 581-586.
37. See Kosnik *et al., Human Sexuality,* p. 203.
38. See Gregory Baum, "Catholic Homosexuals," in *Commonweal,* 99 (1974), pp. 479-481.
39. See Guindon, *The Sexual Language,* p. 344.
40. See Kosnik *et al., Human Sexuality,* p. 211.
41. See Kosnik, *et al.,* p. 215.
42. See Kosnick, *et al.,* p. 215.
43. See Kosnik, *et al.,* p. 216.

CHAPTER 15

1. See the main points of discussion on "Roe vs. Wade" (41 U.S. 113, 93, Supreme Court 705-1973) as it appears in James Humber and Robert Almeder (eds.), *Biomedical Ethics and the Law* (New York: Pflaum Press, 1976), pp. 17-26.

2. See Daniel Callahan. *Abortion: Law, Choice and Morality* (New York: MacMillan, 1970), pp. 448-480. No more recent statistics were available at the time of this writing.

3. See Noonan, *Contraception,* p. 28.

4. John T. Noonan, "An Almost Absolute Value in History," in *The Morality of Abortion,* edited by John Noonan (Cambridge, MA: Harvard University Press, 1970), p. 5.

5. Noonan, *Contraception,* p. 28.

6. Noonan, "An Almost Absolute Value...," pp. 8-9.

7. Noonan, p. 9.

8. Noonan, p. 10.

9. Noonan, p. 11.

10. Council of Ancyra, canon 21 in J.D. Mansi, *Sacrorum Conciliorum nova et amplissima collectio* (Roma, 1961 ed.), 2.5.19.

11. But it must be noted that Tertullian does not accept therapeutic abortion. See Noonan, "An Almost Absolute Value...," pp. 26-32.

12. See Nelson, *Human Medicine,* p. 34.

13. See Nelson, p. 35.

14. See Haring, *Medical Ethics,* p. 76.

15. See Haring, p. 35.

16. See Haring, p. 35.

17. Sixtus V, *Effraenatum* in *Codicis Iuris Fontes,* edited by P. Cardinal Casparri (Roma, 1927), p. 308.

18. See Nelson, *Human Medicine,* p. 35.

19. Code of Canon Law (CIC), #747, p. 220.

20. N.C.C.B., *To Live in Christ Jesus,* p. 23.

21. See Nelson, *Human Medicine,* p. 37.

22. See Nelson, p. 37.

23. See Nelson, p. 37.

24. See Sheldon Cherry, M.D., *Understanding Pregnancy and Childbirth* (New York: Bobbs-Merrill, 1973), pp. 5-9.

25. See Nelson, *Human Medicine,* p. 39.

26. See Leon Eisenberg, "Psychiatric Intervention," in *The Morality of Abortion,* pp. 101-112.

27. See J.H. Edwards, "Amniocentesis," in *Dictionary of Medical Ethics,* edited by A.S. Duncan *et al* (London: Darton, Longman and Todd, 1977) pp. 13-16.

28. See the text as it appears under the following heading: " 'Roe vs. Wade': Decision on Abortion by the U.S. Supreme Court," in *Ethics in Medicine: Historical Perspectives and Contemporary Concerns,* edited by Stanley Reiser *et al.,* (Cambridge: MIT Press, 1977), pp. 401-405.

29. See *Ethics in Medicine,* p. 401.

30. *Humanae Vitae,* par. 14.

31. See Sissela Bok, "Ethical Problems of Abortion," in *Bioethics,* edited by Thomas Shannon (New York: Paulist Press, 1976), pp. 43-46.

32. Thielicke, *The Ethics of Sex,* pp. 226-247; Dietrich Bonhoeffer, *Ethics* (New York: MacMillan, 1955), p. 130, Charles Curran, *Politics, Medicine,*

and Christian Ethics: A Dialogue with Paul Ramsey (Philadelphia: Fortress Press, 1973), pp. 114-131.

33. See Haring, *Medical Ethics*, p. 76.
34. See *Humanae Vitae*, par. 17.
35. See O'Donnell, *Medicine and Christian Morality*, pp. 153-198.
36. See O'Donnell, p. 204.
37. See Callahan, *Abortion: Law, Choice, and Morality*, pp. 448-480.
38. See Callahan, pp. 460-468.
39. See Callahan, p. 467.
40. Nelson, *Human Medicine*, p. 52.
41. See Callahan, *Abortion: Law, Choice, and Morality*, pp. 493-494.
42. See Callahan, pp. 378-383.
43. See Callahan, pp. 384-390.
44. See Callahan, pp. 390-394.
45. See Nelson, *Human Medicine*, p. 58 Cf. Ralph Potter, Jr., "The Abortion Debate," in *Updating Life and Death,* edited by Donald Cutlet (Boston: Beacon Press, 1968), p. 94.
46. See Callahan, *Abortion: Law, Choice and Morality*, p. 456.
47. See Callahan, pp. 451-460.

CHAPTER 16

1. Theodosius Dobzhansky, "Man into Superman: The Promise and Peril of the New Genetics," *Time* (April 19, 1971), p. 33.
2. See Nelson, *Human Medicine*, p. 99.
3. See Nelson, p. 100.
4. See Bruce Hilton, "Will the Baby Be Normal?... And What Is the Cost of Knowing?," *The Hastings Center Report,* vol. 2, n.3 (June 1972), p. 8.
5. See Nelson, *Human Medicine*, p. 101.
6. George Lobo, S.J., *Current Problems on Medical Ethics* (Westminster, MD: Christian Classics, 1974), p. 155.
7. Haring, *Ethics of Manipulation*, p. 191.
8. See Haring, p. 191.
9. See Nelson, *Human Medicine*, p. 107.
10. See Paul Ramsey, "Screening: An Ethicist's View," in *Ethical Issues in Human Genetics,* edited by Bruce Hilton *et al.,* (New York: Plenum Press, 1973), p. 148.
11. See Haring, *Ethics of Manipulation*, pp. 180-181.
12. See Haring, pp. 173-174.
13. See Haring, p. 174.
14. See Nelson, *Human Medicine*, pp. 99-100.
15. In 1976 Patrick Steptoe (a gynecologist at the Oldham and District General Hospital, England) and Robert Edwards (a physiologist at Cambridge University), reported a pregnancy that lasted ten weeks. But the embryo implanted in the oviduct instead of the uterus and was miscarried.

Then it happened. After more than eighty unsuccessful attempts, Steptoe and Edwards produced a full-term pregnancy. The parents were Lesley

Brown of Bristol and her husband John, an employee of British Rail. She was infertile because of blocked oviducts, and surgery had failed to correct the problem. On July 25, 1978, Lesley gave birth to a five pound, twelve ounce baby girl by caesarean section. See P. Gwynne *et al.,* "All about That Baby," *Newsweek* (August 7, 1978), pp. 66-72. See also "Calcutta Woman Has Test-Tube Baby," *Seattle Times* (October 6, 1978), p. A-16.

16. See David Lygre, *Life Manipulation* (New York: Walker & Co., 1979), pp. 30-37.
17. See Nelson, *Human Medicine,* p. 113.
18. See Nelson, p. 114.
19. See Nelson, p. 117.
20. See Nelson, p. 118.
21. See Leon Kass, "New Beginnings in Life," in *The New Genetics and the Future of Man,* edited by Michael Hamilton (Grand Rapids, MI: Eerdmans, 1971), p. 36.
22. See Lobo, *Current Problems in Medical Ethics,* p. 153.
23. See Haring, *Ethics of Manipulation,* p. 200.
24. See Lygre, *Life Manipulation,* p. 26.
25. See Haring, *Ethics of Manipulation,* p. 202.
26. See Haring, p. 202.
27. See Haring, p. 203.
28. See Kass, "New Beginnings," p. 42.
29. See Kass, p. 42.
30. See Paul Ramsey, *Fabricated Man,* p. 92.
31. See Curran, *Contemporary Problems in Moral Theology,* p. 198.
32. See Christopher Lasch, "Birth, Death and Technology: The Limits of Cultural Laissez-Faire," *The Hastings Center Report,* Vol. 2, n. 3 (June 1972), p. 1ff.

Selected Bibliography

Barnhouse, Ruth Tiffany and Urban T. Holmes (eds.). *Male and Female: Christian Approaches to Sexuality*. New York: The Seabury Press, 1976.

Burghardt, Walter, S.J. *Woman: New Dimensions*. New York: Paulist Press, 1975.

Callahan, Daniel. *Abortion: Law, Choice & Morality*. New York: The Macmillan Company, 1970.

Curran, Charles (ed.). *Contraception: Authority and Dissent*. New York: Herder & Herder, 1969.

Dedek, John. *Contemporary Medical Ethics*. Kansas City: Sheed, Andrews, McMeel, 1976.

Doherty, Denis (ed.). *Dimensions of Human Sexuality*. Garden City, N.Y.: Doubleday & Co., Inc., 1979.

Erikson, Erik. *Identity: Youth and Crisis*. New York: W.W. Norton & Co., 1965.

_____. *Childhood and Society*. New York: W.W. Norton & Co., 1966.

Francoeur, Robert. *Eve's New Rib: Twenty Faces of Sex, Marriage and Family*. New York: Harcourt, Brace & Jovanovich, 1972.

_____ and Anna Francoeur (eds.). *The Future of Sexual Relations*. Englewood Cliffs, N.J.: Prentice-Hall, 1974.

Fuchs, Josef, S.J. *Human Values and Christian Morality*. Dublin: Gill & Macmillan, 1970.

Goergen, Donald. *The Sexual Celibate*. New York: The Seabury Press, 1974.

Grelot, Pierre. *Man and Wife in Scripture*. Translated by Rosaleen Brennan. London: Burns & Oates, 1964.

Guindon, Andre. *The Sexual Language*. Ottawa: Univ. of Ottawa Press, 1977.

Hamilton, Michael (ed.). *The New Genetics and the Future of Man*. Grand Rapids, Mich.: Wm. B. Eerdmans Co., 1972.

Haring, Bernard C.Ss.R. *Medical Ethics*. Slough: St. Paul Publ., 1972.

_____. *Ethics of Manipulation*. New York: The Seabury Press, 1975.

Humber, James and Robert Almeder (eds.). *Biomedical Ethics and the Law*. New York: Plenum Press, 1976.

Jewett, Paul. *Man as Male and Female*. Grand Rapids, Mich.: Wm. B. Eerdmans Co., 1975.

Katchadourian, Herant and Donald Lunde. *Fundamentals of Human Sexuality*. New York: Holt, Rinehart and Winston, 1972.

Keane, Philip S.S. *Sexual Morality: A Catholic Perspective*. New York: Paulist Press, 1977.

Kennedy, Eugene. *The New Sexuality: Myths, Fables and Hang-Ups*. Garden City, N.Y.: Doubleday & Co., Inc., 1972.

Kosnik, Anthony *et al. Human Sexuality: New Directions in American Catholic Thought.* New York: Paulist Press, 1977.

Lobo, George, S.J. *Current Problems in Medical Ethics.* Slough: St. Paul Publ., 1974.

Masters, William and Virginia Johnston. *Human Sexual Response.* Boston: Little, Brown & Co., 1966.

May, Rollo. *Love and Will.* New York: W.W. Morton & Co., 1969.

McCormick, Richard, S.J. *Ambiguity in Moral Choice.* Marquette, Wisc.: Marquette Univ. Press, 1974.

McNeil, John P. *The Church and the Homosexual.* New York: Pocket Books, 1976.

National Committee for Human Sexuality Education. *Education in Human Sexuality for Christians.* Washington, D.C.: U.S.C.C., 1981.

National Conference of Catholic Bishops. *To Live in Christ Jesus.* Washington, D.C.: U.S.C.C., 1976.

Nelson, James. *Human Medicine: Ethical Perspectives on New Medical Issues.* Minneapolis: Augsburg Publ. Co., 1973.

_____. *Embodiment: An Approach to Sexuality and Christian Theology.* Minneapolis: Augsburg Publ. Co., 1978.

Neubeck, Gerhard (ed.). *Extra-Marital Relations.* Englewood Cliffs, N.J.: Prentice-Hall, 1969.

Noonan, John T. *Contraception.* Cambridge, Mass.: Harvard Univ. Press, 1965.

_____. *The Morality of Abortion.* Cambridge, Mass.: Harvard Univ. Press, 1970.

O'Connell, Timothy. *Principles for a Catholic Morality.* New York: The Seabury Press, 1978.

O'Donnell, Thomas, S.J. *Medicine and Christian Morality.* New York: Alba House, 1976.

O'Neil, Robert and Michael Donovan. *Sexuality and Moral Responsibility.* Washington, D.C.: Corpus Books, 1968.

Peel, John and Malcolm Potts. *Textbook of Contraceptive Practice.* New York: Cambridge Univ. Press, 1970.

Pittenger, Norman. *A Time for Consent.* London: SCM Press, 1970.

Pyle, Leo (ed.). *Pope and Pill.* London: Darton, Longman & Todd, 1968.

Reiser, Stanley *et al.* (eds.). *Ethics in Medicine.* Cambridge, Mass.: MIT Press, 1977.

Rock, John. *The Time Has Come.* New York: Alfred Knopf, 1963.

Sacred Congregation for the Doctrine of the Faith. *Persona Humana: Declaration on Sexual Ethics.* Washington, D.C.: U.S.C.C., 1977.

Schillebeeckx, Edouard, O.P. *Marriage: Human Reality and Saving Mystery (vols. I & II).* Translated by N.D. Smith. New York: Sheed & Ward, 1965.

Shannon, Thomas (ed.). *Bioethics.* New York: Paulist Press, 1976.

Taylor, Michael, S.J. (ed.). *Sex: Thoughts for Contemporary Christians.* Garden City, N.Y.: Doubleday & Co., 1972.

Thielicke, Helmut. *The Ethics of Sex*. Translated by John Doberstein. Grand Rapids, Mich.: Baker Book Co., 1964.

Whittaker, Peter. *The American Way of Sex*. New York: G.P. Putnam's Sons, 1974.

Index

193